Walter Smith Cox

Questions for the Use of Students

In the Junior Law Class of Columbian University

Walter Smith Cox

Questions for the Use of Students
In the Junior Law Class of Columbian University

ISBN/EAN: 9783337179915

Printed in Europe, USA, Canada, Australia, Japan

Cover: Foto ©Suzi / pixelio.de

More available books at **www.hansebooks.com**

QUESTIONS

FOR THE

USE OF STUDENTS

IN THE

JUNIOR LAW CLASS

OF

COLUMBIAN UNIVERSITY.

BY

WALTER S. COX,

PROFESSOR IN THE LAW DEPARTMENT OF COLUMBIAN UNIVERSITY,
WASHINGTON, D.C.

WASHINGTON, D. C.:

W. H. MORRISON,

LAW PUBLISHER AND BOOKSELLER,

1891.

PHILADELPHIA:
SHERMAN & CO., PRINTERS.

BLACKSTONE.

Section III.

INTRODUCTION.

1. What is municipal law?
2. Into what two branches are the laws of England divided?
3. What is embraced by the unwritten law?
4. What is the common law?
5. What are the general subjects to which it relates?
6. What is the origin of the common law?
7. Where is the common law to be found?
8. What are law reports?
9. What is the difference between the records of judgments and reports?
10. What is the authority of text-books?
11. What are the earliest law reports?
12. What do they resemble in this country?
13. What is the force and value of precedents?
14. What other customary law is there besides the common law?
15. Give example of special customs?
16. What difference between those of which the courts take notice and those which have to be proved?
17. How were customs of the city of London proved?
18. How customs generally?
19. What proof is necessary to establish a binding local custom?
20. Can it prevail against an express statute?
21. What is necessary to make a binding local commercial usage?
22. What was legal memory at common law?

23. What is the effect of a judicial decision establishing a local custom?
24. What other branches of the unwritten law are there besides the common law?
25. What is the civil law and what the canon law?
26. In what courts do they prevail?
27. How are they parts of the unwritten law?
28. What authority do the common law courts exercise over the others?
29. What is the written law?
30. Can an English court pronounce a statute void?
31. How is it in this country?
32. What are public and what are private statutes?
33. What the difference in their effect?
34. Who are bound by a private statute, and how is it proved?
35. How are public statutes divided?
36. How far does the preamble control the interpretation?
37. What is stated in the text to be a general guide in the interpretation?
38. How are penal statutes to be construed, and give example?
39. What are statutes against fraud, and remedial statutes, and how do they differ from penal?
40. What is the rule as to the different parts of a statute?
41. How if there be a saving or proviso contradictory to the body of the statute?
42. What is the effect of a statute plainly inconsistent with the common law or a previous statute?
43. What is the effect of repealing a statute which itself repeals a prior statute?
44. Can a statute be good which binds in terms subsequent legislatures or parliaments against its repeal?
45. What is the difference between such and legislative grants, as *e.g.*, exemptions from taxation to corporations?
46. How are statutes on the same subject (*in pari materia*) to be construed?
47. If a statutory offence is not punished while the statute is in force, can it be afterwards?

48. If a statute inflicts a penalty for an act without declaring it unlawful in terms, does that make it unlawful?
49. If a statute creates a new offence and prescribes a penalty, can any other be inflicted?
50. Suppose it adds a new penalty to one existing at common law, does that exclude the old one?
51. What is the force of a statute to fix the interpretation of a former one?
52. In what case can a statute act retrospectively?

BLACKSTONE.

Book I, Chapter I.

1. What is the difference between absolute and relative rights of person?
2. What between rights of persons and rights of things?
3. What are called the absolute rights of Englishmen?
4. What does the right to personal security involve?
5. Is this recognized in an unborn child?
6. Is an injury to personal security from mere negligence recognized as an actionable wrong?
7. What may one do in defence of life and limb?
8. What will be justified by mere battery or threats?
9. What are offences against the reputation?
10. What is an offence against personal liberty, and what amounts to false imprisonment?
11. What is duress, and what its effect upon bonds and contracts?
12. What are the relative rights of father and husband?
13. What causes of action grow out of a negligent injury to a minor child or wife?
14. What is the father's remedy for the seduction of a minor child, and what is the name of the action?
15. In case of the death of wife or child from negligence, what remedy has husband or father?

16. Has the child or wife any remedy for injuring, disab
killing father or husband?
17. What are known as the guarantees of the rights of En
men?
18. What does Magna Charta provide as to personal libert
as to the rights of property?
19. What is there analogous to it in our laws?
20. What was the next important public act?
21. What was the occasion of the petition of right?
22. What provision in it was engrafted on our Constitutio
23. What was the habeas corpus act, and what did it prov
to personal liberty?
24. What was the declaration of rights of 1688?
25. What does it contain in common with our Constitutio
26. What was the last of the guarantees, and what does i
tain that is followed in our Constitution?
27. On the hearing of a habeas corpus, what is inquired in
determined?
28. What is the power of the Federal courts to issue a h
corpus where a party is imprisoned under process
State court?
29. What is the right of eminent domain, and how is it
cised?
30. How far must the compensation required by the Co
tion go? does it extend to consequential injury?

BLACKSTONE.

Book I, Chapter IX.

1. What was the Sheriff, anciently?
2. How is he now appointed?
3. How was he formerly elected?
4. How, generally, in this country?
5. What were the Sheriff's judicial duties?

6. Has he any such in this country?
7. What is his power as to preservation of the peace?
8. What is his main ministerial duty?
9. In inquisitions of damages, what are his duties?
10. What was the office of coroner?
11. What are his duties?
12. What are his duties in case the Sheriff is party to a suit?
13. What was the Justice of the Peace originally?
14. When did they begin to be called Justices?
15. What are his duties, and when ministerial and when judicial?
16. In what case is he liable to action?
17. What is the general jurisdiction of Justices in this country?
18. What is the Constable, and what his duties?

BLACKSTONE.

Book I, Chapter X.

1. What is allegiance, natural and local?
2. Can natural allegiance be renounced by the law of England?
3. How in this country?
4. Can a subject or a citizen acquire a foreign character, and for what purpose?
5. What period in our history fixes the nationality of American citizens?
6. What are the disabilities of aliens as to property?
7. Can a native-born subject or citizen inherit through an alien?
8. How if two brothers are natives, but the father an alien; can one brother inherit from the other?
9. Can an alien acquire and hold lands?
10. What becomes of them?
11. In case of the death of an alien before office found, what becomes of the land?
12. What if the alien convey it away?

13. What can an alien merchant do?
14. Can an alien acquire and dispose of personal property?
15. Can he take a mortgage?
16. Could he buy in at a sale under the mortgage and hold?
17. Can he bequeath his property?
18. What becomes of it in case of intestacy?
19. How is the alien's disability removed?
20. What is a denizen, and how must one be naturalized?

BLACKSTONE.

Book I, Chapter XIV.

1. What was the effect of a general hiring at common law?
2. What is now considered the effect?
3. Is any warning necessary to terminate the relation?
4. If the servant leave in the middle of the month or quit without cause, what can he claim?
5. How if he is dismissed without cause?
6. How if he leaves for good cause?
7. How if he is dismissed for good cause?
8. How if the contract is terminated by mutual consent?
9. When the contract is for a certain time, what is the rule?
10. If wrongfully discharged, can he sue at once, or must he wait until the term has expired?
11. Is the master bound to provide medical attendance for domestic servants?
12. Is he bound to give his servants a character?
13. Are disparaging characters to servants actionable libels?
14. What may a master do for a servant and not for a stranger?
15. How far is a master bound by contracts made by a servant in his name?
16. How if I deal with a tradesman for ready money and he furnishes goods to the servant on my credit?
17. If I sometimes send cash and sometimes not?

18. What is the master's responsibility for torts of the servant?
19. If I employ a man to repair my house, is he a servant for whose negligence I am responsible?
20. How as to sub-contractors and sub-servants?
21. Is the master liable to one servant for injuries from neglect of another?
22. What is the tendency of modern decisions on this subject?

Chapter XV.

1. What is marriage in the view of the common law?
2. What is the first requisite to a valid marriage?
3. How many kinds of disabilities are there?
4. What are canonical disabilities, and what their effect?
5. What are the civil disabilities?
6. At what age may a man and woman respectively marry?
7. What right has one marrying under age when he or she arrives at majority?
8. What right of disaffirmance has the one who married at proper age?
9. How is this an exception to general rules?
10. How does want of reason affect the marriage?
11. What form of contract is sufficient for a valid marriage?
12. By the law of what place is the validity of the marriage determined?
13. How if parties go there to evade the law of their domicil?
14. How is marriage dissolved?
15. How many kinds of divorce are there?
16. What was the effect of a divorce *a vinculo?*
17. For what causes was it granted?
18. Divorces *a mensa et thoro*, for what causes?
19 What is alimony?
20. By what law, in this country, is the validity of a divorce determined?
21. What is the effect of marriage on contracts before marriage, between husband and wife?

22. What on her power to contract with others or to contract with her husband, and their power to convey to each other, to testify for or against each other?
23. What is the effect of the husband's outlawry?
24. Of his abandonment of the wife?
25. What rights does he acquire as to her personal chattels?
26. How where she holds as joint tenant with another?
27. How as to her paraphernalia?
28. What property does he acquire as to her choses in action?
29. How if he dies before reducing them to possession?
30. How if he survive her?
31. How if he then dies?
32. What acts amount to a reduction to possession?
33. How of transfer of stock?
34. How of indorsement of note for value?
35. How of voluntary assignment in bankruptcy?
36. What is the wife's survivorship?
37. What are equitable choses in action, and what power has the husband over them?
38. Suppose he has to resort to a Court of Equity to get them into possession, what is the practice of the Court in such cases?
39. What proportion is settled to the wife's use?
40. What is this right of the wife called?
41. Suppose the husband makes an assignment of the wife's equitable choses in action, which does not, of itself, amount to a reduction to possession, what are the wife's rights?
42. Suppose the husband dies after the assignment, what is the result?
43. How in case of assignment of the wife's reversionary interest in stocks?
44. What interest does a husband acquire in the wife's chattels real?
45. Can he bequeath them?
46. Can he sell and convey them?
47. Are they liable for his debts?
48. If he grant a rent charge out of them, will it survive him?

49. What interest does he acquire in his wife's freehold estates?
50. Suppose she be tenant *pur autre vie* and dies before the *cestui que vie*, what has the husband?
51. What interest does he acquire in her fee-simple estates?
52. Can the husband's interest in the wife's estate be levied upon?
53. What power of disposition has the wife over her estate, personal and real?
54. What is the usual form now of settling property on a married woman?
55. What is its effect?
56. What are clauses against anticipation in such settlements?
57. How can her separate estate be made liable for her debts?
58. What is the force of ante-nuptial agreements to settle property on the wife?
59. Are such agreements good against creditors?
60. What post-nuptial agreements can be made?
61. Suppose a wife to join in a deed with her husband, to convey her title, which contains covenants, is she bound by them?
62. Can she execute a bond or contract to convey?
63. What interest does a wife acquire in her husband's personal estate?
64. What in his real?
65. In what property does she acquire dower?
66. How if husband alien without her concurrence?
67. What are deeds of separation, and what the usual form?
68. What effect have they on the wife's control of her property?
69. What are the husband's liabilities for his wife?
70. What effect has his death on his liability?
71. What effect has her death?
72. How as to her choses in action not reduced in her lifetime?
73. What debts is he liable for, contracted during marriage?
74. Suppose the husband to forbid tradesmen to supply his wife, what can the latter do?
75. If the husband, in fact, supply necessaries, can a tradesman recover for articles furnished necessary in quality?

76. If the wife is forced to leave her husband, what authority does she carry with her?
77. What precautions must a tradesman take in dealing with her?
78. How as to allowances paid and not paid?
79. What is his liability for her torts?
80. What for fraudulent contracts, false representations, etc.?

BLACKSTONE.

Chapters XVI, XVII.

1. What is the father's common law obligation to maintain an infant child?
2. Is there a difference, and if so, what, between a father's and a husband's liability?
3. If a child resides with its father, has a tradesman any right to supply the child necessaries on the father's credit?
4. Who determines what are necessaries?
5. If the child has left the father, what would be the presumption of authority to the child to procure necessaries?
6. If the child were driven away, how?
7. What is the parents' duty as to education?
8. Does the child's own fortune make any difference at common law?
9. How is it in Courts of Equity?
10. Is the mother under any obligation to support the child?
11. What is the parents' right as to the services of the child?
12. How if the child be allowed to go with the mother in case of separation?
13. How if allowed to go and work for himself?
14. What right of action may parents have founded on this right?
15. In what sense is a parent guardian?
16. Does it give him any control over the property of his children?

17. What may he do in defence of his children?
18. When do his authority and liability for them cease?
19. What is a bastard?
20. What effect had subsequent marriage on the legitimacy of a bastard?
21. What were the disabilities of a bastard?
22. Could he inherit from his known mother?
23. Could he from his brother who was a bastard?
24. Could a bastard's children inherit from *his* father?
25. Could they inherit from *him?*

Chapter XVII.

1. How many kinds of guardianship were there, and what called?
2. Who were guardians by nature and nurture?
3. Guardianship in socage, was what?
4. What were testamentary guardians, and by what law authorized?
5. To what age does this guardianship continue?
6. Is a female infant's guardianship terminated by her marriage?
7. Would any guardian be appointed anew for her?
8. Does the guardian acquire any estate in the ward's property?
9. Can the guardianship be assigned?
10. Can the guardian make any profit out of the estate of the ward?
11. What are the capacities of infants at different ages?
12. How must an infant sue?
13. What is his legal capacity for criminal offences?
14. Can he be charged with negligence?
15. Can he execute deeds or bonds, or bills of exchange, or negotiable notes?
16. Can he act as trustee?
17. What contracts may he make?

BLACKSTONE.

CHAPTER XVIII.

1. How are corporations divided first?
2. What is a sole and what an aggregate corporation?
3. What are the advantages of a corporation over a mere partnership or voluntary association?
4. How are aggregate corporations divided generally?
5. How lay corporations?
6. What are eleemosynary corporations?
7. If all its members are ecclesiastics, can it be a lay corporation?
8. How are civil corporations divided?
9. What are public corporations?
10. What are canal and railroad corporations?
11. Can a corporation be created by agreement between a number of individuals?
12. How are they created?
13. What new mode of creating them is there in this country?
14. What is the first essential to their existence?
15. In what form of words are they created at common law?
16. What is the mode of proceeding in this country?
17. What is meant by the capital stock?
18. What is a share of the capital stock in the hands of the individual member?
19. What kind of property is it, personal or real?
20. What are said to be the incidents of a corporation?
21. What is the meaning of having perpetual succession?
22. How, at common law, was the succession kept up?
23. What were the rights of members as to election and a motion?
24. What is the difference in modern business corporations?
25. What words are necessary to the conveyance of a fee simple to a corporation?
26. Of what acts is a corporation incapable?
27. Can it commit a tort and be indicted?

28. Can it act without a head?
29. Can it receive property without a head?
30. How does it execute deeds?
31. How does it acknowledge deeds of lands?
32. What formality is now considered necessary in the making of contracts, and what was the ancient rule?
33. What is the rule as to voting, and what kind of voting will legally control the action of the corporation?
34. What is the distinction between officers *de jure* and *de facto?*
35. What is the general power of corporations with reference to things not forbidden?
36. Can it avoid its own act as in excess of its powers?
37. How are suits brought by and against corporations?
38. What power has a corporation out of the State in which it was created?
39. Can it be sued elsewhere, at common law?
40. What is the general condition of the statute law on this subject in this country?
41. In what cases could corporations sue and be sued in the Federal courts?
42. What is the rule now?
43. What were the statutes of Mortmain, and at what were they aimed?
44. Have they been generally re-enacted in this country?
45. Could corporations take as devisees?
46. What was the visitation of corporations?
47. Who was visitor of ecclesiastical corporations?
48. Who of eleemosynary corporations?
49. What was the power of a visitor?
50. Can this power be delegated, and how is it done?
51. What was the decision of the Supreme Court in the case of Dartmouth College *vs.* Woodward, 4 Wheat. 518?
52. Are civil corporations subject to visitation?
53. How are they restrained within their proper sphere?
54. How are municipal corporations affected by legislation?
55. Can a private corporation be dissolved by act of legislature?
56. How can it be?

57. What are the two kinds of proceedings against a corporation to declare it unlawful and dissolved?
58. What is the difference between them, and what the judgment in the two cases?
59. In whose name must such proceedings be instituted?
60. Can its forfeiture of charter be taken advantage of collaterally?
61. Can it forfeit property, or any of its privileges, unless that be adjudged directly?
62. What were the common law consequences of dissolution as to property? How is it now?
63. Can a corporation, holding property, convey it in fee simple, so that its reverter to the original owner, on its dissolution, would be prevented?

BLACKSTONE.

Book II, Chapters I, II, and III.

3 *Kent, Lect.* 52.

1. What is real property?
2. What is embraced by the term "land?"
3. What by "tenement?"
4. How are hereditaments divided?
5. What is the maxim as to the extent of ownership of land?
6. What passes by a grant of it?
7. What are the incorporeal hereditaments?
8. Which of them do not exist in this country?
9. What is the definition of an easement?
10. What is the difference between an easement in gross and appurtenant?
11. What are the two estates called affected by the easement?
12. What was the common law division of commons?
13. What the effect if the tenant bought part of the common land?

14. Common appurtenant was what?
15. Common of vicinage, what?
16. Common of piscary was what?
17. What rights at common law had owners of land bordering on rivers?
18. Free fishery was what?
19. Several fishery?
20. Is there a common law right in any one to haul the seine on the land of any one on a river?
21. Is there a right to tow boats along the river shore?
22. What is a way?
23. How does it arise?
24. What is a way in gross?
25. Can it be assigned or transmitted to heirs?
26. How does it differ from a common in gross?
27. A way of necessity is what?
28. Suppose a trustee sells land to which there is access only over his own land; does a way of necessity arise?
29. If a man sells all his own land except a part in the centre does he have a way of necessity over it?
30. How is a right of way extinguished?
31. What is a public way of necessity?
32. Does the same rule apply to private ways?
33. When a river or other natural object is called for as the boundary of land, to what point does the land extend?
34. If land be gradually washed from one side to the other of a river, to whom does it belong?
35. If violently, to whom?
36. Between low and high tide-water mark, to whom does the land belong?
37. Below tide-water, what is the boundary of land calling for the river?
38. How of a grant of land bounded by the highway?
39. When a public road is condemned through private property, what is taken?
40. To whom does timber in the highway belong?

41. What right have adjoining proprietors over a party wall?
42. What rights have parties in streams running through their properties?
43. What length of enjoyment gives title to an easement, in this country?
44. How may it be lost?
45. Was there any common law obligation to fence lands?
46. Was it trespass for one's cattle to stray into unfenced lands?
47. What right have I to open a window looking over my neighbor's land?
48. What remedy has he?
49. What was the English doctrine of ancient lights?
50. What is the law in this country?
51. How is an easement acquired by dedication?
52. What is a license?
53. What kind of interest does it give?
54. In what cases is it irrevocable?
55. In what case is rent an incorporeal hereditament?
56. If I lease for years, is the rent such?
57. What were the different kinds of rents?
58. What was the rent charge?
59. How must it be created?
60. For how long a term may one grant a rent?
61 How have they been used to evade the usury laws?
62. *Are they within the statute of uses?*
63. *If an estate be to A, to the use that B might receive a rent for the use of C, what estates had they?*
64. *If a rent charge, held by one for his life, be granted away to another without naming his heirs, and the grantee dies, what becomes of the rent?*
65. How are ground rents or charges generally created in this country?
66. How were rent charges extinguished?
67. What was the effect of entry into part of the land, or recovery by title paramount?
68. *Was rent the subject of tenure?*
69. *Could it be held of another and escheat?*

70. What is the nature of rent on long leases in this country?
71. Is it a hereditament?
72. What are ground rents?

BLACKSTONE.

Book II, Chapters IV, V, and VI.

3 Kent, Lect. 53.

1. On the introduction of feuds, what was understood by fealty?
2. Of whom is all land supposed to be held in England?
3. What was doing homage?
4. What was the Court Baron?
5. What were the *pares curiæ*.
6. For what term or estate were feuds first granted?
7. What was the motive or consideration of the grant?
8. What were the restrictions on the early grants?
9. What was meant by the term *tenure?*
10. What were the general divisions of ancient tenures?
11. What was the most important of tenures by uncertain service?
12. What were the obligations of the tenure by Knight service?
13. What were its incidents, and what were aids, reliefs, and primer seisin, wardship, marriage, fines for alienation and escheat?
14. What were escuages?
15. What was enacted by the Stat. 12 Chas. II?
16. What were socage tenures, and what their division?
17. What is an example of base, uncertain service?
18. What were villeins and their disabilities?
19. What was a manor?
20. What was the origin of copyhold estates?
21. What was the evidence of title of a copyholder?
22. What was the difference between copyholder and freeholder?
23. How did the base services of pure villeinage disappear?

24. What evils grew out of the subinfeudations and the granting of manors by the Lords?
25. How was it corrected, and what were the enactments of the Stat. *Quia Emptores*, 28 Edw. I.?
26. Can there be any new manors since that statute, and why not?
27. What are allodial lands?
28. What is the tenure in this country?
29. What is the relation of land-owners to the State?
30. What is escheat in this country?

BLACKSTONE.

Book II, Chapter VII.

4 *Kent, Lect.* 54.

1. What is the highest estate in land that a subject can have?
2. What is the original meaning of the term *fee?*
3. What does the term *freehold* comprehend?
4. What formality accompanied the grant of a feud for life?
5. What was it called, later?
6. What were the objects of this formality?
7. What was the efficacy of livery of seisin?
8. What is a fee-simple estate?
9. Must the fee always be represented by some one?
10. What words are necessary to make a fee?
11. Will *heir*, or to one *or* his heirs, suffice?
12. Will a conveyance to one and his assigns, or to one forever, do?
13. How of a grant to one and his children forever?
14. How of a grant to one and his heirs for the life of another?
15. What exceptions to the rule?
16. What expressions will suffice in a will?
17. What is the principle attribute of a fee-simple estate?
18. How of conditions restricting control?

19. As to alienation, enjoyment, waste, dower, etc.?
20. Can the owner restrain his own power of alienation?
21. Alienation is of how many kinds?
22. Can the owner protect the estate against involuntary alienation by creditors.
23. How can improvidence be provided against?
24. Can a man settle his own property in this way?
25. What class of people are an exception to the rule?
26. What are examples of qualified or base fees?
27. What is the difference between these and an estate to one and his heirs for the life of another?
28. What power of disposition has the owner over a base fee?
29. What was the conditional fee at common law?
30. What the construction of the courts as to *heirs of the body?*
31. What the effect of birth of issue?
32. What the course of descent, if donee did not alien?
33. What was the statue *de donis?*
34. What its effect on conditional fees?
35. On the estate of the donor in reversion?
36. What kind of an estate was an entail?
37. How many kinds of estates tail?
38. If tenant in tail male has a grandson descended from a daughter, can he inherit?
39. If tenant has estates in tail male and tail female, which can a daughter's son inherit?
40. What words are necessary to make an estate tail?
41. What passes by deed to one and his issue?
42. What was a gift in frank-marriage?
43. If it be to husband and wife and the heirs of his body begotten on his wife, what estate passed?
44. If to husband and wife and the heirs of their bodies, what?
45. How, if it be a man and woman not married?
46. To a man and the wife of another man?
47. If to two husbands and their wives?
48. What is a gift to one and his heirs male, or female?
49. What were the incidents of an estate tail?
50. What were the evils of entails?

51. How were they remedied?
52. What is the substitute for entails in England and what in this country?

—

BLACKSTONE.

Book II, Chapter VIII.

4 *Kent, Lect.* 55.

1. What was the earliest of the freehold estates?
2. What was the position of a tenant for life?
3. How is the estate created?
4. If a grant be to one generally, is it for his or grantor's life?
5. Can one life estate be carved out of another, and how?
6. Suppose life tenant grant to remainderman for his life, what is the effect?
7. Is it a surrender?
8. What are the incidents of a life estate, as to waste, estovers, etc.?
9. If the tenant dies before harvest where do the crops go?
10. How with tenant *par autre vie?*
11. How of an estate during covertures where there is a divorce?
12. How if tenant during widowhood marry, or forfeit by treason?
13. To what does the doctrine of emblements apply?
14. How as to sub-tenant of tenant for life?
15. How if tenant for life terminate his estate by his own act?
16. *If land be granted to tenant for life, remainder over, incumbered by a mortgage, how is the mortgage to be borne between life tenant and remainderman?*
17. *In what proportion are they to pay off?*
18. *Suppose life tenant to pay it off, what are his rights?*
19. What would be waste, voluntary and permissive?
20. What if the house were burned by tenant's neglect or carelessness?
21. What is an estate tail after possibility of issue extinct?

22. Suppose tenant in tail grow to be 80 or 90 years old, does the estate become such?
23. Suppose husband and wife, tenants in tail special, procure a divorce, are they tenants after possibility of issue extinct?
24. What are the incidents?
25. Suppose the tenant attempts to convey a fee, does he forfeit?
26. Can he exchange with tenant for life?
27. What was an estate by the curtesy?
28. What was necessary?
29. What the effect of birth alone?
30. What kind of seisin must wife have had?
31. When is the wife seised in fact, if the land is occupied by a tenant when she inherits?
32. When is actual seisin unnecessary?
33. Why was it necessary at all?
34. What birth of issue is necessary?
35. What estate had a husband before the wife's death?
36. Has he curtesy in a trust estate?
37. What kind of equitable estate must wife have?
38. How if the seisin is in trustees for her use?
39. How as to qualified fees and estates on condition which is broken?
40. How does tenant by curtesy forfeit; does he by adultery, or by wife's treason?
41. What is dower?
42. What is the first requisite to dower?
43. How if the marriage be voidable for consanguinity, by the ecclesiastical courts?
44. How if actually avoided?
45. How if an idiot marry?
46. How if the wife is an alien?
47. How if the husband is a joint tenant?
48. What kind of seisin in the husband is sufficient?
49. *How if the husband die before entry for condition broken?*
50. *How if tenant of freehold hold over until after the husband's death?*

51. How if there be a lease for life which does not terminate before the husband's death?
52. How of a transitory seisin and what are examples of such?
53. How if the husband have a life estate, remainder to another, remainder to husband and his heirs in fee?
54. Is the wife dowable of rents, commons, etc., and under what circumstances?
55. Does dower attach to land acquired before but owned after coverture?
56. Can a husband defeat the dower by aliening the land?
57. How could the wife release her dower at common law?
58. How does she now?
59. Is she dowable of an equity of redemption?
60. How, in this country?
61. Where she is dowable, how is she bound, as to the mortgage debt?
62. How is she dowable where the mortgage is for years?
63. How many kinds of dower and what were they?
64. What is the widow's quarantine?
65. What is the right of dower before assignment?
66. Can she enter before assignment?
67. Can she remain in the homestead after the forty days, if the heirs refuse to assign her dower?
68. What is the effect of assigning the dower?
69. Who must assign and what is the remedy for refusal?
70. *What is the relation of widow and heir after assignment?*
71. How must dower be assigned if the property is not divisible?
72. How of property owned in common with others by the husband?
73. In what case are two widows to be endowed out of the same land?
74. What is the maxim "*dos de dote peti non debet,*" and how does it apply?
75. How is dower assigned in case of exchange of lands?
76. On what valuation is dower to be computed with reference to general enhancement of property?

77. How as to improvements made by husband or heir?
78. Suppose the widow be evicted by title paramount, what is her remedy?
79. Does she hold under the heir or her husband?
80. How may dower be barred?
81. How prevented from ever attaching?
82. What acts would forfeit her dower?
83. How if she aliened the lands?
84. What is a jointure?
85. What is the usual method of barring dower in this country?

BLACKSTONE.

Book II, Chapter IX.

4 *Kent, Lect.* 56.

1. What is an estate for years?
2. What was the original status of a lessee for years under the feudal system?
3. How could the lessee's estate be defeated by the landlord?
4. How long must the estate be, to be an estate for years?
5. What is a year; a half year?
6. What is a month in law?
7. When so many days' notice is required, when must the day of service be excluded; when included?
8. What amount of certainty is required as to the duration of the term?
9. What of a lease for so many years as one shall live?
10. How does this differ from a life estate?
11. How of a lease for twenty years if one shall live so long?
12. What is the difference between *term* and *time*, as to leases?

13. Can a lease be made to commence at a future day?
14. What is necessary to perfect the estate for years?
15. What difference between entry and livery?
16. What has the tenant before entry?
17. Can this interest be surrendered?
18. Can it be enlarged by grant of the reversion?
19. In what form must a lease be made?
20. At common law must the lease be in writing?
21. What does the Statute of Frauds provide?
22. What is letting upon shares?
23. Is tenant for years entitled to emblements?
24. How if he is lessee under tenant for life?
25. What is tenant's obligation as to repairs?
26. What the landlord's?
27. Is dilapidation an excuse to the tenant for leaving, or a defence against action for rent?
28. How if landlord covenant to repair?
29. Can tenant dispute the landlord's title?
30. What may he show as to it?
31. What is the consequence of his disputing it?
32. What is disclaiming, attorning, etc., and what the consequences to the tenant?
33. Is a mere refusal to pay rent equivalent to a disclaimer?
34. *What if landlord evict tenant from part of the premises?*
35. *What of annoyances materially interfering with the tenant's enjoyment of the property?*
36. *What of eviction under a paramount title?*
37. What of mere trespass by strangers?
38. Suppose one to go into possession under a lease without signing it, is he liable for rent?
39. *What implied covenants are there in a lease?*
40. *What on lessee's part, from words "yielding and paying," etc.?*
41. *What do express covenants generally relate to?*
42. *How is a covenant to renew satisfied?*
43. If at election of lessee, when must he exercise his election?
44. What effect has destruction by fire on covenant to pay rent?

45. Is the lease forfeited by non-payment of rent?
46. *Must the tenant seek the landlord or the reverse, in the payment of rent?*
47. *How if the lease provides for re-entry on failure to pay?*
48. *What is necessary in such case to enable the landlord to re-enter?*
49. What difference is there between a condition that the lease shall be forfeited, and a condition that landlord may re-enter on failure to pay?
50. What if landlord does not enter?
51. If tenant contract to repair and the house is burned down, what is his obligation?
52. How if the house be destroyed by lightning or the public enemy?
53. If he covenants to keep in repair and the house is out of repair when he takes it, how is it?
54. Who is liable to third person for accidents resulting from the ruinous state of the premises?
55. What is an assignment and what an under-lease?
56. How is a covenant not to assign broken?
57. Suppose it be not to assign lessee's interest or any part thereof?
58. *What is the difference between transferring the whole land for part of the term, and transferring part of the land for the whole of the term?*
59. What is landlord's relation to assignee and to sub-tenant?
60. Can landlord and sub-tenant look to each other for anything?
61. Upon an assignment, what are the obligations of the assignee and what his rights against the landlord?
62. *To the benefits of what kind of covenants is either entitled?*
63. *Is the lessee exempted from the express covenant by the assignment?*
64. *How as to implied covenants?*
65. *Is assignee liable for any breach of covenant after his reassignment?*
66. *What important rule is there about taking a mortgage of a lease?*
67. How far does the form or language make an assignment or under-lease?

68. How if tenant lease for his whole term?
69. *Must an assignment be in writing?*
70. *How if tenant for less than three years assign verbally?*
71. *What amounts to a waiver of forfeiture?*
72. *If a breach be a continuing one, how far would one waiver go?*
73. *How does equity deal with forfeitures?*
74. *If reversioner sells to several, how is the rent payable?*
75. *If vendor and vendee agree upon the apportionment, how does this affect the tenant?*
76. *How where the reversion descends to different persons?*
77. How as to time, as when lessor dies in the midst of a current quarter, etc.?
78. *How are implied surrenders made?*
79. *Can under-tenants surrender to lessor?*
80. *Can surrender be by parol?*
81. Can tenant surrender to the prejudice of sub-tenant?
82. How does merger of the lease take place?
83. Does one term merge in one succeeding it?
84. When does a term merge in a term?
85. What will prevent a merger?
86. *Must the two estates be held in the same right?*
87. *How of a term held by husband in right of his wife, and an inheritance in his own right?*
88. *What was the English practice as to long terms?*
89. *What were terms to attend the inheritance?*
90. *What if one bought with notice of incumbrances, could he then take a term to attend, etc.?*
91. What can tenant take away with him at the termination of his lease?
92. What are fixtures?
93. What is the distinction between agriculture and trade?
94. What becomes of a lease for years, on tenant's death?
95. Does it pass by a devise of all lands and tenements?
96. How is it affected by a judgment? *Fieri facias?*
97. What is an estate at will?
98. Can tenant at will assign?
99. What are his rights as to emblements?

100. What right has tenant to determine, in the middle of his quarter, etc.?
101. What determines the estate?
102. In what case do tenancies at will exist now?
103. What is an estate from year to year?
104. In what cases does it arise?
105. What does a lease for one year and so on from year to year, amount to?
106. How if one go into possession under an agreement for a lease never executed and pays rent?
107. How if the rent be payable monthly or if the property be let generally at so much a month?
108. What is a tenancy by the month or quarter?
109. If one becomes tenant from year to year by holding over, on what terms does he hold?
110. How if he goes in under a void lease?
111. How does a general letting of lodgings operate?
112. What is the peculiarity of the lease from year to year?
113. What notice to quit is necessary in the case of a tenancy for years?
114. How of a tenancy from year to year?
115. On what day must the notice end?
116. What is the most advisable form of notice?
117. Should the notice be in the alternative, as, *e.g.*, to quit or pay higher rent, would it suffice?
118. How if landlord accepts rent accruing after expiration of the notice to quit?
119. What notice is necessary in case of a renting from month to month, etc.?
120. How should the notice be given?
121. What may the landlord do after expiration of the notice?
122. What is a tenancy at sufferance?
123. How is it terminated?
124. What converts it into an estate from year to year?
125. What remedy is provided by Stat. 4 Geo. II, as to holding over after notice by landlord to quit?
126. What by 11th Geo. II, as to holding over after notice by tenant of his intention to quit?

BLACKSTONE.

Book II, Chapter X.

4 *Kent, Lect.* 57, 58.

1. What are the conditions in law?
2. What is an express condition?
3. What two kinds? Give examples.
4. What difference is there between them?
5. How, if condition precedent becomes impossible?
6. How, if condition subsequent becomes impossible?
7. What is the difference between a limitation and a condition? Examples.
8. What is the important difference as to the actual termination of the estate?.
9. Does breach of this condition subsequent of itself terminate the estate?
10. Is there any difference between freehold estates and those for years in this respect?
11. To whom could the right of entry for condition broken be reserved?
12. How was the right of entry treated at common law?
13. What was the effect of entry for breach of conditions in deed?
14. How, in case of conditions in law?
15. What was a conditional limitation?
16. If performance be tendered and refused, what is the consequence?
17. How if it be payment of money?
18. How, if mortgage debt be tendered and refused?

MORTGAGE.

19. How many kinds of mortgages were there?
20. What is the nature of the mortuum vadium?
21. Can the defeasance be in a different instrument from the grant?
22. Why were mortgages formerly for terms of years?

23. What is the usual provision in mortgages about retention of possession by the mortgagor?
24. What kind of interest does this give to the mortgagor?
25. What may the mortgagor do with the property, subject to the rights of the mortgagee?
26. What is the equity of redemption?
27. How long will this right be enforced, and in analogy to what rule?
28. How do courts of equity treat any agreement in or contemporaneous with the mortgage to waive this right of redemption?
29. How do courts of equity look upon a mortgage?
30. Will a mortgagor be allowed to commit waste?
31. Who are allowed this equity of redemption?
32. Can one entitled to redeem do so on payment of less than the whole debt?
33. *How can a judgment creditor redeem a leasehold?*
34. *On redemption, if mortgagee has been in possession, what will be exacted of him?*
35. What credits will he be entitled to?
36. How as to permanent improvements?
37. Can the mortgagor part with the equity to the creditor after executing the mortgage?
38. *What is a conditional sale with a right to repurchase?*
39. Is there any equity of redemption?
40. What strictness is required in complying with the condition?
41. *What are the obligations of heir and executor, respectively, in relation to mortgaged property?*
42. *What rights has the heir as to application of the personal estate?*
43. What are the rights of the mortgagee after forfeiture?
44. How if the property be under lease?
45. What is the right of foreclosure?
46. If there was no covenant for payment of the debt, had the mortgagee any further remedy?
47. *If mortgagee sell for a fair price after foreclosure, can he sue for the deficiency?*

48. What is the general practice of the courts, in this country, as to foreclosure?
49. What the modern form of mortgage, as to selling?
50. What the still more modern substitute for the mortgage?
51. Who must be made parties in a suit for foreclosure, and why?
52. How is the mortgagee barred of his foreclosure?
53. Is a reconveyance necessary when a mortgage is paid off?
54. What is the effect on the mortgage of an assignment of the debt itself?
55. What is the difference, as to remedies and the bar of time, between the mortgage and the debts secured by it?
56. *What was the English doctrine as to tacking further advances to the original mortgage debt?*
57. Under what circumstances will future advances be secured by the mortgage as against intermediate incumbrances?
58. What was the English practice of tacking mortgages?
59. What is an equitable mortgage?
60. Against whom will it prevail?
61. What is a vendor's lien?
62. Against whom will it prevail?
63. What amounts to a waiver of the vendor's lien?
64. What were the Statutes, Merchant and Staple?
65. What was the tenant by elegit?
66. What was the rank of these interests as estates?
67. Can an absolute deed be shown by parol to be intended as a mortgage?

BLACKSTONE.

Book II, Chapter XI.

4 *Kent, Lect.* 58.

1. What is a remainder, and how does it differ from a reversion?
2. What is the first estate which precedes a remainder called?

3. How many estates may be carved out of a fee?
4. Can there be any remainder after a fee?
5. If a term for years be created to begin in futuro, or a freehold, under the Statute of Uses, will it be a remainder?
6. How at common law could a freehold be created to take effect in future?
7. Why must there be a particular tenant?
8. What is the relation of the particular estate to the remainder?
9. Will an estate at will support a remainder, or why not?
10. When must the title of the remainder pass from the grantor?
11. How in the case of a contingent remainder?
12. When must the remainder become vested? Why?
13. Does the reason apply to remainders for years?
14. Is it a remainder if it does not take effect before or at the expiration of the preceding estate?
15. Can an estate be a remainder which goes into effect by abridging the particular estate?
16. What is such an estate?
17. Can a remainder be limited after a life estate in case another remainder in fee does not take effect?
18. Cross-remainders are what?
19. What are the two kinds of remainders?
20. What is the essence of the vested remainder?
21. If an estate be to A for life, remainder to B for A's life, is it vested?
22. If to A for life, remainder to such uses as he may appoint, and in default of such appointment to B, is B's remainder vested or contingent?
23. How if to A for life, remainder to his children, present and future?
24. How if it be to A, if or when he attains 21 years of age, and the intermediate estate is disposed of?
25. How if to trustees and their heirs until A attain 21 years of age, and then to him?
26. Under what two general heads may contingent remainders be classed? Examples.

27. How of a remainder to children unborn and the case of a posthumous child?
28. *What has the certainty of enjoyment to do with the question of vested or contingent?*
29. What is too remote a contingency?
30. If the estate be to A for 80 years, remainder to B on the death of C, is it a vested or contingent remainder?
31. If an estate be to one for life, remainder to his heirs, is it a contingent remainder?
32. What kind of particular estate is necessary to support a contingent remainder?
33. How is a remainder affected by the destruction of the particular estate, or its invalidity?
34. *Can the remainderman take advantage of a condition subsequent?*
35. How is a remainderman affected by a particular tenant incurring forfeiture?
36. *How does the disseisin of the particular tenant affect the remainderman?*
37. *How if disseisee's right of entry is gone?*
38. What is the contrivance of a trust to preserve contingent remainder?
39. If a contingent remainder in fee be given, where is the fee before the contingency happens?
40. How in the case of future uses and executory devises?
41. Could contingent remainders be conveyed, devised, etc.?
42. The rule in Shelly's case is what?
43. What were supposed to be the reasons for it?
44. How are intervening estates between the life estate and inheritance affected?
45. How if the two estates are not created by the same deed?
46. *How if, by virtue of a power in the same deed, the inheritance is given to the heirs of the tenant for life?*
47. *Does the rule apply even if the intention appears to be different, when the technical words are used?*
48. *How as to executory trusts?*
49. *What are the exceptions to the rule?*
50. How when the two estates are of a different character?

51. What is a reversion?
52. At common law was there a reversion upon the grant of a fee?
53. What statute changed this, and how?
54. What are the incidents of a reversion?
55. What passes by a grant of the reversion?
56. What effect has the assignment of rent on the reversion?
57. Suppose one convey for life, with remainder to himself and heirs, what estate has he?
58. How are reversions transferred?
59. What is the difference between reversion after an estate for years and after a freehold?
60. How must the latter be transferred?
61. *Is a reversion subject to a levy of an execution?*
62. What remedies has reversioner for injuries to the freehold?
63. What is merger?
64. Can a term merge in a term?
65. What kinds of estates are subject to merger?
66. Is the larger estate increased by the merger?
67. Will it take place if there be an intervening estate?
68. *In what cases will it take place if the two estates are held in different rights?*
69. *How if legal and equitable estates meet in the same person?*

BLACKSTONE.

Book II, Chapter XI.

4 Kent, Lect. 60.

1. What are executory devises?
2. What is their effect on the free disposition of the fee simple?
3. What are the three kinds of executory devises?
4. Why can a freehold be devised to commence *in futuro?*
5. What becomes of it in the meanwhile?
6. Why could not a fee be limited after a fee by deed?
7. Why could not a term for years be limited for life with remainder over, by deed?

8. What restriction is there upon the power to limit them by will?
9. What is the main difference between contingent remainders and executory devises?
10. As to the power of the present tenant to destroy them, what?
11. Within what time must an executory devise take effect in possession, and why?
12. How if the contingency on which it is to take effect may occur within the time or not?
13. *If a devise be made to one in fee, but if he should die without issue, over to another, what construction is given to the words "without issue?"*
14. Is such a devise over a good executory devise?
15. *How do the courts sustain the devise over?*
16. *How of a devise to one generally and then over, if he should die without issue?*
17. When an estate is devised, to commence *in futuro*, what becomes of the profits in the meanwhile?
18. What of the income of personal estate so devised?
19. Can an executory devise be assigned, devised, or inherited?
20. Was there any limit at common law to the number of lives running at the same time, during which the executory devise was suspended?
21. In what case was this question decided?
22. What was held as to the accumulation of the income meanwhile?
23. What statutory enactment was the result of that case?

BLACKSTONE.

Book II, Chapter XII.

4 *Kent, Lect.* 64.

1. How was a sole owner said to hold?
2. How did several owners hold?
3. How is a joint tenancy created?

4. What are the unities of a joint tenancy?
5. How of an estate to A and B and the heirs of A?
6. If the owner of the fee die first, what is the result?
7. How if it be to A and B and one moiety to the heirs of each?
8. What of unity of time?
9. What if the estate be to A, remainder to the heirs of B and C, and B dies first after A?
10. *How as to conveyances under the Statute of Uses?*
11. *How of a devise to the use of the children of A?*
12. What is the nature of the seisin of joint tenants and coparceners?
13. How of an estate to man and his wife in fee?
14. How, if a man and woman be joint tenants and afterwards marry?
15. Can either dispose of an undivided moiety so as to sever the tenancy?
16. How is this survivorship prevented in a grant?
17. Can a joint tenant devise his interest?
18. Is his wife entitled to dower, as against the survivor?
19. If a joint tenant make a will, and himself survive, does his will operate?
20. How of mortgages made before survivorship?
21. Do they bind his grantee?
22. Is joint tenancy favored by the courts?
23. How of partnership property?
24. How is joint tenancy destroyed?
25. What is the effect of a conveyance by one to a stranger?
26. How if one of three convey to a stranger?
27. How if one of three releases to one of the others?
28. What are the advantages and disadvantages of a severance?
29. What if one joint tenant grant away for the life of his co-tenant?
30. For what is a joint tenancy useful now?
31. What is the difference between granting to A and B and their heirs, and to A and B and the survivor, and the heirs of the survivor?
32. How did an estate in coparcenary arise?

33. What kind of coparcenary is there in this country?
34. What unities has this estate?
35. How if one coparcener dies leaving daughters?
36. What is the difference in the seisin from that of joint tenants?
37. How is the coparcenary severed?
38. What was hotchpot?
39. What unities has tenancy in common?
40. How may it have others?
41. How is the tenant seized?
42. What is the effect of his death?
43. How can he deal with the property?
44. How can part of the fee in an undivided interest be held in common and the rest in joint tenancy?
45. How of a grant to several men or several women and the heirs of their bodies?
46. How of a grant to two; one moiety to each?
47. How of a devise to two, equally between them?
48. Can one of several owners grant away a part, by metes and bounds?
49. By what conveyance can one joint tenant convey to another? Why?
50. How of a tenant in common?
51. How do the acts of one joint tenant affect the others, and what acts?
52. What of release, entry, reservation of rent in lease, etc.?
53. How as to joinder in suits?
54. In what do tenants in common join?
55. If in a lease, how is it considered?
56. How is the possession of one considered with reference to the other?
57. How if one actually exclude the other?
58. How is tenancy in common destroyed?
59. What is the effect of a conveyance by one tenant in common to a stranger?
60. What remedy had joint tenants or tenants in common against the others for repairs?
61. How is a partition compelled?

BLACKSTONE.

Book II, Chapters XIII and XIV.

4 Kent, Lect. 65.

1. What is necessary to constitute a perfect title?
2. Why is mere possession called a form or degree of title?
3. Define the difference between the mere possession, apparent and real right of possession?
4. What was the effect of death of disseisor in possession on the rights of disseisee?
5. What was the difference between possessory actions and writs of right, as to bar by lapse of time?
6. What was a discontinuance by tenant in tail?
7. What its effect on the rights of the heir?
8. What was the effect of judgment in a possessory action against the plaintiff?
9. When the real owner can neither enter nor maintain a possessory action, what has he?
10. Can his mere right be assigned?
11. What is title by descent?
12. What is consanguinity? How many kinds?
13. What is lineal, and what collateral?
14. What is the heir apparent, and what the heir presumptive?
15. Has either any title in the life of the ancestor?
16. What must an heir show to establish title by descent?
17. Give an application of the rule?
18. How is the seisin necessary for descent acquired?
19. In exchanges, if both die before entry what is the consequence?
20. How, if one die?
21. What is seisin in law, and what seisin in fact?
22. Is the former sufficient to transmit title?
23. If the ancestor had a tenant for years or life, what was necessary to make actual seisin in the heir?
24. What seisin of incorporeal hereditaments is necessary?
25. What is the first rule of descent?
26. What is the second rule?

27. What is the third?
28. How, where there were daughters only?
29. What the fourth rule as to representation? Examples.
30. What is taking *per stirpes*, and what *per capita?*
31. Where the deceased had several daughters and one of them had died leaving sons, what was the rule?
32. What was the fifth rule?
33. What was meant by the first purchaser?
34. Grandfather, father, and son; the father had purchased. To whom could the estate go?
35. If the grandfather, how?
36. To whom could one purchasing anew transmit?
37. What was a *feudum novum* to be held *ut feudum antiquum?*
38. How, if in fact the land descended to the propositus?
39. What is the sixth canon of descent?
40. How was the count in the common and how in the civil law?
41. What is the ground of the difference?
42. On what ground is a nephew preferred to an uncle when both are in the same degree?
43. Is the descent to collateral heirs immediate or through the common ancestor?
44. What is the difference, in relation to ancestors, between kindred of the whole and the half blood?
45. What is the ground of the rule which confines the inheritance to the whole blood?
46. What is the seventh rule, and what the grounds of it?
47. How, if lands descended on the mother's side?
48. What is hotchpot?

Chapter XV.

49. What is title by purchase? Examples.
50. If a man devise to his heirs, how do they take?
51. How, if with limitations different from what the law would create?
52. If an estate be given to A, remainder to the right heirs of B, how do the latter take?

53. What is the difference between taking by purchase and descent, as to transmission to heirs?
54. As to debts and incumbrances?
55. What was title by escheat?
56. What were bastard *eigne* and *mulier puisne?*
57. What was escheat through corruption of blood?
58. What is the difference between forfeiture and escheat?
59. How may there be forfeiture without escheat, and how *vice versa?*
60. What was the effect of corruption of blood as to descent through the party attainted?
61. What is the law of escheat in this country?

BLACKSTONE.

Book II, Chapters XV, XVI, XVII, XVIII.

1. What is title by occupancy?
2. Why cannot an estate *pur autre vie* descend to heirs?
3. Why not escheat?
4. What was general, and what special, occupancy?
5. What did the Statute 29 Chas. II enact as to estates *pur autre vie?*
6. What did the Statute 14 George II enact?
7. How does the law of occupancy apply to incorporeal hereditaments?
8. What is title by prescription, and how is prescription different from custom?
9. In how many different ways does one claim title by prescription?
10. What limit upon the right to prescribe was imposed by Statute 32 Henry VIII?
11. To what kind of property does the title by prescription apply?

12. To what kind of estate?
13. Can it apply to any rights that cannot be created by grant?
14. Can it apply to rights which must be created by record?
15. To what class of heirs must an estate claimed by prescription descend?
16. How far back must an immemorial usage, as the foundation of rights, formerly, have been traced?
17. What is the present rule?
18. What is the uniform rule in this country?
19. On what analogy is it founded?
20. What was the consequence of alienation in mortmain?
21. By what kind of alienation did a tenant of a particular estate incur a forfeiture?
22. What is the consequence of such forfeiture?
23. What was the consequence of a feoffment in fee by tenant in tail?
24. What was the consequence of alienation by deed in fee by particular tenants of rents, reversions, or other estates which lie in grant?
25. How if one attempt to convey a larger estate than he has by deeds operating under the Statute of Uses?
26. What is disclaimer by a tenant, and what its effect?
27. Is there a forfeiture by excessive alienation in this country?
28. What is waste, voluntary and permissive?
29. What its consequences at common law and under the Statute of Gloucester?
30. What is title by execution?
31. What eqecution affected real estate?
32. Under what law was real estate made subject to *fieri facias* in this country?
33. How is personal property affected by *fieri facias*?

BLACKSTONE.

Book I, Chapter XIX and Part of XX.

4 *Kent, Lect.* 67.

1. What power of alienation had a feudatory under the feudal system?
2. Whose consent was necessary?
3. How far could the lord alien his reversion or seigniory?
4. What was attornment?
5. What was enacted by Statute of Queen Anne in reference to attornments?
6. What was the first step in the direction of free alienation?
7. When and how did one first acquire the right to sell his lands?
8. What was the purport and operation of the Statute *Quia Emptores?*
9. What is the effect of that statute upon fee simple alienations at this day?
10. By what statute was the power given to charge lands with debts?
11. By what statute was the power of devising given?
12. What restraint was there imposed on the right of alienation by the Statute 32 Henry VIII?
13. What was the effect under that statute of a conveyance by one out of possession?
14. What is the importance of the rule in making out a chain of title in ejectment?
15. Who are incapable of valid alienation?
16. What interests may be alienated?
17. Can a contingent remainder?
18. Can a person *non compos mentis* avoid his own deed?
19. What was the old rule?
20. What can his heirs do after his death?
21. What can a minor do in the way of avoiding his own deed?
22. What is duress, and what its effect upon deeds?

23. Can a feme covert alien her property?
24. Can she purchase real estate?
25. Can she disaffirm such purchase, and when, and can her heirs?
26. What was the original form in which title to a feud passed?
27. What was the origin of deeds?
28. What their original form?
29. What is a deed, and how many kinds are there?
30. How far is a consideration necessary to a deed?
31. Does want of consideration affect title under a deed accompanied with livery?
32. How many kinds of consideration are there?
33. With reference to whom is a valuable consideration necessary to the validity of a deed?
34. How is a voluntary deed affected by the Statute of 13 Eliz. against fraudulent conveyances?
35. On what must the deed be written?
36. Was writing necessary to the transfer of real estate at common law?
37. By what statute was it made necessary?
38. What was the origin of seals?
39. What acts could not be done without a deed?
40. Were they necessary to the transfer of corporeal hereditaments?
41. By what law, if any, did deeds ever become necessary to the transfer of real estate in England?
42. How is it in this country?
43. What is a seal?
44. What are the several parts of a deed of conveyance?
45. If a description of property is inconsistent, how is it to be construed?
46. What is embraced by lands or houses in a conveyance?
47. When is an exception bad?
48. What is the habendum?
49. When is the habendum bad?
50. What is the tenendum?
51. Is it now in use?

52. What was the reddendum, and how does it differ from an exception?
53. What was warranty by the old common law, and what rights did it give?
54. In what case was a warranty implied before the Statute *Quia Emptores?*
55. What is the effect of the Statute of *Quia Emptores* upon the warranty implied by the word "*dedi?*"
56. What was the origin of express warranties?
57. How far did they effect the heir?
58. How many kinds of warranty are there?
59. What was the effect of lineal warranty upon the heir?
60. What was collateral warranty?
61. What was the ruling of the courts as to the bar of collateral warranty?
62. What was the nature of the obligation of warranty?
63. Is the old form of warranty still in use, or what supersedes it?
64. What are covenants of title, and what are the usual covenants of both parties to a deed?
65. What is meant by covenants running with the land?
66. What covenants do and what do not, run with the land, and why the difference?
67. By what acts is the covenant to warrant and defend, broken?
68. How is it affected by trespasses of third persons?
69. Under the old form of warranty, what was recovered by the person warranted, when evicted?
70. What is the measure of damages now in an action for the breach of covenant of warranty?
71. How in case of partial eviction?
72. What is special warranty?
73. How far is reading necessary to the validity of a deed?
74. How many kinds of delivery of a deed are there?
75. From what time does a deed operate?
76. Is attestation necessary to a deed?
77. What acts avoid a deed?
78. How many kinds of common law conveyances are there?
79. What was a feoffment?

80. What was the process of conveying by feoffment?
81. To whom must livery of seisin have been made on a grant for years with remainder in fee?
82. How on the conveyance of a reversion on an estate for years?
83. How many kinds of livery are there?
84. When was livery in law good, and what was continual claim?
85. What was disseisin?
86. What estate did a man acquire by disseisin?
87. What two kinds of disseisin are there?
88. What was the effect of the disseisor's death?
89. What was disseisin by election?
90. What is a gift?
91. What is a grant?
92. What is a lease, and what its operative words?
93. How does a lease differ from an assignment?
94. What is necessary to a lease for life?
95. What did the Statute 29 Chas. II provide as to leases?
96. What is an exchange?
97. What are the essentials of exchanges as to the quantity of the estate?
98. Is livery of seisin necessary?
99. Is entry?
100. What if one party dies before entry?
101. Is there implied warranty, and what its effect?
102. How does it differ from other warranties?
103. What word was essential to an exchange?
104. Can an exchange be with two distinct deeds?
105. What is partition?
106. Is there any warranty implied in partition?
107. What are the derivative conveyances?
108. What is the appropriate language of a release?
109. How does a release operate to enlarge an estate?
110. What must the release have to make the release operative?
111. How does a release pass an estate?
112. How does it pass a right?
113. How does it operate by way of extinguishment?

114. How by way of entry and feoffment?
115. What is a confirmation?
116. What is a surrender?
117. Can a life estate be surrendered to a tenant for years?
118. Can a term for years be surrendered to the tenant for the succeeding term?
119. Is livery of seisin necessary to a surrender?
120. If particular tenant and remainderman or reversioner unite in a deed in fee, how is it construed?
121. What is a defeasance?

BLACKSTONE.

Book II, Part of Chapter XX.

4 *Kent, Lect.* 61.

1. What gave rise to uses in England?
2. What was imported by a feoffment by one to the use of another?
3. What are the names of the respective parties?
4. What originally was the estate of the feoffee to uses?
5. Who were originally bound by the uses?
6. What was held as to the estate of the cestui que use?
7. What was a shifting or secondary use?
8. What was a springing use?
9. What was a future or contingent use?
10. Within what time must a shifting or springing use take effect?
11. What is a springing use taking effect through a power?
12. What is a resulting use?
13. What was the effect of a deed of feoffment without consideration and expressing no uses?
14. What was the effect of such a deed expressing the uses?
15. What the effect of bargain and sale or a covenant to stand seized to uses, with or without consideration?
16. If one granted an estate to the use of some one at a future time, what became of the intermediate use?

17. What evils resulted from the system of uses?
18. What statuté was passed to remedy the evils?
19. Recite the statute?
20. What is the general object of the statute?
21. To what case does it apply?
22. What is the effect upon common law estates?
23. How could a legal freehold be made to arise *in futuro* under this statute?
24. How a fee limited after a fee?
25. How did this statute affect the jurisdiction of equity?
26. To what cases did the law courts hold the statute inapplicable?
27. What was the consequence, and how did the court of equity resume its jurisdiction over the subject?
28. Was a trust estate subject to dower or curtesy?
29. What effect has the trustee's alienation upon the trust?
30. What did the Statute 29 Charles II provide as to trusts?
31. What trusts do not require to be evidenced by writing?
32. Give examples of resulting trusts?
33. What is a trust estate general?
34. What are executed and executory trusts?
35. How do courts of equity construe and give effect to a contract for the sale of land?
36. What is a covenant to stand seized to uses?
37. What consideration is sufficient for it?
38. What is a bargain and sale?
39. What consideration is necessary to it?
40. How does the statute operate upon it?
41. What did the Statute 27 Henry VIII require as to bargain and sale?
42. What is a lease and release?
43. What other deeds are there besides conveyances of land?
44. What is a single bill?
45. What is a bond with condition?
46. On whom and what is it binding?
47. What if the condition be impossible when it is executed or in violation of some positive law?

48. What if it be to do something criminal *per se?*
49. What if it become impossible?
50. If the bond is forfeited, what is recoverable?
51. What is a fine?
52. What is a common recovery?

Stat. 27 Henry VIII.

Where any person or persons stand or be seized, or at any time hereafter shall happen to be seized, of and in any honors, castles, manors, lands, tenements, rents, services, reversions, remainders, or other hereditaments, to the use, confidence, or trust of any other person or persons, or of any body politic, by reason of any bargain, sale, feoffment, fine, recovery, covenant, contract, agreement, will, or otherwise, by any manner, means whatsoever it be; that in every such case, all and every such person and persons, and bodies politic, that have or hereafter shall have any such use, confidence, or trust, in fee-simple, fee-tail, for term of life or for years, or otherwise, or any use, confidence, or trust in remainder or reverter, shall, from henceforth, stand and be seized, deemed and adjudged in lawful seizin, estate, and possession, of and in the same honors, castles, etc., to all intents, constructions, and purposes in the law, of and in such like estates as they had or shall have in the use, etc., of or in the same, and that the estate, title, right, and possession that was in such person or persons that were, or hereafter shall be, seized of any lands, tenements, or hereditaments, to the use, etc., of any such person or persons, or of any body politic, be from henceforth clearly deemed and adjudged to be in him or them that have, or hereafter shall have, such use, confidence, or trust, after such quality, manner, form, and condition as they had before, in or to the use, confidence, or trust that was in them.

4 *Kent, Lect.* 62.

1. What is a power?
2. What are the ordinary powers operating under the Statute of Uses?

3. How does a power of revocation and appointment, when executed, operate?
4. Who were the parties to a power?
5. What other powers are there besides those of appointment and revocation?
6. What are powers appendant and appurtenant?
7. What collateral and in gross?
8. By what instrument may a power be created?
9. If I grant to A in fee, with a power of future disposition, does that create a power?
10. What of a devise to A generally, with a general power of disposition?
11. What of a devise for the life of the devisee, with power to appoint the fee?
12. What of a devise to such uses as a person may appoint, and in default of such appointment to that person and his heirs?
13. If that person then convey in fee, is he passing his estate or executing his power?
14. What is the difference between a devise to executors to sell and a direction that they shall sell?
15. What becomes of the title in either case before sale?
16. If the power is to appoint in fee, what estate must be given to the first grantee or devisee?
17. Within what time must the power of future appointment be exercised?
18. What is the difference, in this respect, between an estate derived under the power of appointment and an executory devise?
19. In case of a devise to such uses as may thereafter be appointed, and in the meantime to A, is A's estate vested or contingent?
20. By what persons may powers be executed?
21. What difference, in this respect, between femes covert and infants?
22. If a power be given to several, in what cases will it survive on the death of one or more?

23. Can a power be assigned?
24. When a power of appointment is executed, how does the appointee take?
25. Can a general power be exercised in favor of the donee himself?
26. Is such power equivalent to an estate in property?
27. If an appointment be to A to the use of B, what estate is created in either?
28. If the power is to be exercised by will, can it be done by deed, and *vice versa?*
29. Is a general power to appoint for any estate exhausted by an appointment of less than the fee simple?
30. If one owns property and has a power to appoint other property, by will, would a general devise of his property be an exercise of his power?
31. In executing a power can a power of revocation be reserved?
32. To what title does the new estate, created by the power, relate?
33. How far does the relation back to the original deed affect intervening rights?
34. How was a power affected by disseisin, or a conveyance by fine or feoffment of the land?
35. Where one had a general power of appointment, what effect did its exercise have in making the property liable for his debts?
36. If it is made the donee's duty to exercise the power for the benefit of others, can the courts enforce its exercise?
37. What is meant by an illusory appointment?
38. What device, in the way of powers, was resorted to to prevent dower?
39. What remedy is there for a defective execution of a power?
40. Can the non-execution of a power be remedied?
41. How is a power extinguished?

BLACKSTONE.

Book II, Chapter XXIII.

4 *Kent, Lect.* 68.

1. What interest in land could be devised before the reign of Henry VIII?
2. How were lands virtually devised by creating a use?
3. How was this practice affected by the Statute of Uses?
4. When was the Statute of Wills made, and what did it enact?
5. What effect had the Statute of Charles II upon the power to devise?
6. What exception was there in the Statute of Wills, and what its object?
7. Who are capable of devising and of being devisees?
8. If a man devise to his heirs, how do they take?
9. What did the Statute of Frauds provide as to wills?
10. What is a sufficient signing?
11. What is a sufficient witnessing of the signature?
12. Must the witnesses subscribe in the testator's presence?
13. What is his presence?
14. Was a legatee competent to attest the will, and was a creditor?
15. What was the effect of their incompetency, and what the remedy provided by the statute?
16. What title must devisor have in order to pass land by his will?
17. What property of the testator does a general devise pass?
18. Does it pass property acquired afterwards?
19. Does it pass property held in joint tenancy?
20. If a joint tenant make a will and survive his co-tenant, does the will pass the property?
21. Can the possibility of his survivorship be devised?
22. What facts amount to an implied revocation?
23. What if the man marry the woman to whom he has devised?
24. What will be an implied revocation of a woman's will?

25. What effect will a subsequent change of seisin of the property have upon the will?
26. What if testator convey away and take a deed back to himself?
27. What if the deed be inoperative for informality?
28. What effect has a mortgage?
29. What effect would foreclosure of the mortgage or a purchase of the equity of redemption have upon a devise of a mortgage?
30. Will accidental cancellation revoke a will?
31. Is entry of devisee necessary to perfect his title?
32. What effect has death of the devisee in the lifetime of the testator?
33. Is it different if his heirs are named?
34. Where does the property covered by a lapsed legacy go?
35. How in case the devise is void?
36. What will pass by a general devise of a testator's estate?
37. What will pass by a devise generally on condition that devisee pay debts?
38. Give examples of estates created by will, *by implication*.
39. If testator devise in technical language as to a man for life, remainder to the heirs of his body, would a fee tail pass if the testator declared his intention that devisee shall not dispose of the property for longer than his life?
40. Where there are repugnant clauses in a will, which prevails?

BLACKSTONE.

Book II, Chapters XXIV, XXV, XXVI, XXIX.

1. What are chattels, real and personal?
2. What are choses in action?
3. What property in wild animals can one acquire?
4. How and when is property in wild animals protected?
5. What property can one have in the elements?
6. What are examples of special property?

7. How can personal property be settled, and for what interest?
8. How if property which perishes in the using be bequeathed to one for life?
9. How of such a general bequest of the residue, embracing perishable property?
10. How if chattels be given in tail?
11. What right has a remainderman as to securing the property?
12. Can chattels be held in joint tenancy?
13. How is the ownership of partners?
14. What is title to personalty by occupancy?
15. What title can one acquire to goods of foreign enemies by capture?
16. What is title by accession?
17. If I mend my carriage with another's materials, whose are they?
18. If chattels be annexed to the freehold, whose are they?
19. If one makes my leather into shoes, whose is it?
20. If one makes my rye into whisky, whose is it?
21. What is title by confusion of goods?
22. What are the rules in different cases?
23. What is title by succession?
24. What is title by forfeiture?
25. What is title by judgment?
26. What is the rule of transit *in rem adjudicatum?*
27. What is a gift?
28. How is it perfected?
29. How is it delivered, if a chose in action?
30. How, if money in the hands of an agent?
31. Is a gift revocable?
32. What gifts are void in law?
33. What if a man gives property on which his creditors could not levy execution?
34. What is a *donatio causa mortis*, and what is necessary to perfect it?
35. What is the subject of a *donatio causa mortis?*
36. How do these gifts differ from legacies?
37. How do they resemble them?

BLACKSTONE.

Book II, Chapter XXX.

1. What is an executory contract?
2. What are specialty, and what parol contracts?
3. How many parties must there be to a contract?
4. How does it differ from a promise?
5. What is a chose in action?
6. How do debts differ from other choses in action?
7. Are they assignable at common law?
8. How are they now, practically, assignable?
9. Give examples of implied contracts?
10. What is a feme covert's capacity to contract?
11. What a minor's?
12. Can a minor execute a bond or negotiable bill?
13. How, if for necessaries?
14. Will intoxication avoid a contract?
15. Can the contracting party set it up?
16. What is duress which avoids contracts?
17. What is consideration?
18. What effect has its absence upon a contract?
19. How many kinds are there?
20. What kind is necessary to sustain a contract?
21. Will a promise suffice to sustain a promise?
22. Is marriage sufficient?
23. Is a moral obligation?
24. Is a pre-existing debt?
25. Is the debt of a minor sufficient to sustain a promise when he comes of age?
26. Is a debt contracted by a feme covert sufficient to sustain a promise made after coverture?
27. What amounts to a valuable consideration?
28. Is a past or executed consideration sufficient?
29. In what cases may it be?
30. In what case is a previous request implied?

31. In what case is a valuable consideration conclusively presumed?
32. What is a sale?
33. In what cases may one pass title, which the purchasers need not inquire into?
34. What is market overt?
35. What is a sale in market overt, and what its effect?
36. What is the law touching market overt in this country?
37. Can I sell what is not in existence?
38. What is a potential existence?
39. What, if a horse happens to be dead at the time of its sale?
40. What, if I contract to sell things to be manufactured?
41. How is a sale completed?
42. When does the right of property pass by a sale?
43. What right has the seller as to payment?
44. What, if payment be not made immediately?
45. Is payment of earnest necessary at common law?
46. Upon sale, what are the rights of parties as to possession?
47. What if a buyer tenders price?
48. What does the Statute of Frauds provide upon this subject?
49. How does it affect the common law as to passing the title?
50. If I buy so many bushels of wheat out of a larger mass, when does the property pass?
51. At whose risk is the property?
52. What warranty is there on a sale of chattels?
53. How does the vendor's possession affect the question of warranty?
54. How if a trustee or executor sell?
55. What warranty of quality is implied by law?
56. How if an article is sold by sample?
57. What is the buyer's remedy if goods do not correspond with the required quality?
58. What in case of an express warranty of quality?
59. What is bailment?
60. What are the different classes?
61. What is a depositum?
62. What a mandatum?

63. What a loan or commodatum?
64. What a pawn or pledge?
65. What are the different degrees of diligence required of a bailee in these cases?
66. What is a common carrier?
67. What is his obligation, and what that of a private carrier?
68. What kind of property have these different bailees in the subject of the bailment?
69. What action can they maintain?
70. What property has the bailor?
71. Can both bailor and bailee sue for injury to the chattels?
72. Is a loan of money a bailment?
73. What are the elements which determine the rate of interest?
74. What two classes of contracts grew out of them?
75. What interest is allowed on contracts in which the principal is put at hazard?
76. What are contracts of this kind?
77. What are bottomry or respondentia bonds?
78. What is insurance?
79. What is a life insurance?
80. What is a policy of insurance?
81. To whose benefit does it enure?
82. What securities have creditors through insurance?
83. What are gambling policies?
84. What wagering policies?
85. What legislation was there on this subject?
86. What is an annuity?
87. Will exorbitant interest in the form of an annuity be allowed?
88. Will a contract, made elsewhere and legal there, but usurious here, be enforced here?
89. What is a bill of exchange?
90. What are the parties to it named?
91. How does it operate in the payment of debts of remote parties?
92. What is a promissory note?
93. To whom may it be payable?

94. What is meant by its negotiability?
95. When did they become negotiable?
96. How do foreign and inland bills differ?
97. What is an acceptor?
98. What an indorser?
99. Which party to a note or bill is considered the principal debtor?
100. What is the obligation of the drawer and indorser?
101. How is a negotiable note transferred?
102. Is want of a valuable consideration a good defence to a promissory note?
103. What is protest of notes and bills?
104. In what cases is it necessary?
105. What notice is necessary in order to hold an indorser?
106. Who must give the notice, and when?
107. What is the effect of the omission to give notice?

BLACKSTONE.

Book II, Chapter XXXII.

1. How old is the power to bequeath personalty?
2. What was the ancient law on this subject?
3. When could a man dispose of all his personalty?
4. What became of the personalty on the owner's death intestate?
5. What was provided by the Statute, West., 13 Edward I?
6. What by the Statute 31 Edward III?
7. What obligation was imposed upon administrators by this statute?
8. To whom must administration be granted under these several statutes?
9. To what court was the administrator responsible?
10. How did the ecclesiastical courts acquire jurisdiction over the probate of wills?

11. What subjects in this connection are determined by them?
12. By what law are they governed?
13. Who is capable of making a testament?
14. Can a married woman?
15. What kind of consent of her husband is necessary?
16. What is a testament?
17. What are nuncupative wills, and when are they valid?
18. What form is sufficient for a testament?
19. What amounts to cancellation?
20. What to revocation?
21. Is a verbal revocation sufficient?
22. What amounts to an implied revocation?
23. What is an executor, and who may be one?
24. Who is entitled to administer on a wife's estate?
25. By what law is the nearness of kin computed?
26. What are the differences between executors and administrators at common law?
27. How is it in this country?
28. What is to be done if an executor or administrator dies without completing the administration?
29. What if the executor died before the testator?
30. What is an executor *de son tort?*
31. What are his rights and liabilities?
32. What are an executor's duties?
33. What was done if the effects of an intestate were in different counties?
34. What is the force of letters of administration in this country?
35. What is an ancillary administration?
36. What is the executor's duty as to inventory and appraisement?
37. In what order were debts to be paid?
38. How of debts due the Crown, or due a State in this country?
39. To what preference, if any, is an executor entitled as creditor?
40. What effect followed from the appointment of a debtor as executor by his creditor?
41. What preference could executor give to creditors?
42. How is the law in this country?

43. What is a legacy?
44. Could executors safely pay legacies as against creditors, and when?
45. How many kinds of legacies are there?
46. What is a demonstrative legacy?
47. What is abatement, and to what kind of legacies does it apply?
48. What is ademption?
49. Does it affect pecuniary legacies?
50. What advantage has a demonstrative over a specific legacy?
51. And what over a pecuniary legacy?
52. Is a bequest of £100 in Consols, or of a mourning ring of the value of £5, a specific or pecuniary legacy?
53. Is a legacy by a husband to a wife, in consideration of her release of dower, subject to abatement?
54. What is satisfaction by legacy?
55. Under what circumstances will a bequest by a debtor to his creditor amount to satisfaction?
56. From what date does a will of personalty speak?
57. What property of the testator is embraced in a general bequest of all his property?
58. When does a legacy lapse?
59. If one of several joint tenants, legatees, die in the testator's life, does the legacy lapse?
60. How if they are tenants in common?
61. How if the bequest be to a class, as to children?
62. How if the legacy be to one if he attains the age of 21, and he die before that?
63. How if the legacy be given absolutely, but payable at the age of 21 years?
64. How if the legacies, in the two cases, are charged on land?
65. When is the legacy considered due and payable by the executor?
66. From what time does it bear interest?
67. How of a bequest of a body of a fund?
68. In what cases will a money legacy bear interest from testator's death?

69. What became of the residue after paying debts and legacies?
70. What is the rule now?
71. When was the legatee's title to the bequest perfect?
72. What does the Statute of Distributions provide?
73. What is the difference in the course of distribution of personalty and the descent of realty?
74. What is the difference as to representation?
75. What is the doctrine of distribution *per stirpes?*
76. What *per capita?*
77. To what cause does it apply?
78. What is hotchpot?
79. By what law is distribution to be made in regard to property in a different place from the domicil of the testator?
80. How as to real estate?
81. What is to be done with the balance in case of ancillary administration?

BLACKSTONE.

Book III, Chapters I and II.

1. What are the remedies by act of party?
2. How far does the right of self-defence go?
3. May one forcibly defend a stranger from assault?
4. What is the right of recaption?
5. Can it be exercised by force?
6. Can one enter another's premises to recover goods?
7. If one recover his goods forcibly, can they be recovered from him again because of the force?
8. What is the right of entry?
9. Can one, having such right, use force?
10. Suppose I forcibly eject an intruder from my house, which he has occupied in my absence, what right of action has he?
11. If I enter upon a wrong-doer may I forcibly hold against him?

12. If I peaceably gain possession of a part of my house, may I forcibly occupy the rest?
13. If my tenant holds over and I enter and take possession in his absence, can I sue him, in trespass for re-entry?
14. If I enter on my land, unlawfully held by a tenant, can he sue me in trespass?
15. What is the sum of the rule against forcible entries?
16. At common law, could a party ejected by force, who held wrongfully, recover the possession from the true owner?
17. What is the private remedy for a nuisance?
18. What is a nuisance, public or private?
19. How may one abate a private nuisance?
20. Can it be done with breach of peace?
21. Can one tear down a wall, built too high, on a neighbor's ground?
22. What is the remedy of distress?
23. To what was it incident?
24. What is a rent-charge?
25. What a rent-seck?
26. For what is a distress used?
27. What may be seized under a distress?
28. Could the goods of a stranger, being on the land?
29. What exceptions are there to the rule?
30. How of a stranger's cattle, on the land?
31. How of a guest's goods, in an inn?
32. How of a boarding-house?
33. How of a horse at a livery stable?
34. How of beasts of the plough?
35. How was distress made?
36. Can it be after the lease expires?
37. Where could it be made?
38. Can landlord break open the door?
39. What is done with the goods distrained?
40. If they be legally taken, can they be retaken?
41. What is a replevin?
42. What is accord and satisfaction?
43. When does it apply; before or after breach of contract?

44. Is an accord a sufficient defence?
45. What is arbitration and award?
46. What are the remedies by the operation of law?
47. What is remitter?

BLACKSTONE.

Book III, Chapters III and IV and Part VII.

1. What is a court?
2. When is a judge a court?
3. How are courts generally divided?
4. What is a Court of Record?
5. What weight had a record?
6. What is the Court of a Justice of the Peace?
7. What are Inferior Courts?
8. What persons are necessary to the operation of courts?
9. What is an attorney-at-law, and who can have one?
10. What was the lowest court known to the common law?
11. What the next?
12. What was the County Court?
13. What was the Aula Regis?
14. Into what courts was this divided?
15. What powers had the Court of King's Bench?
16. What jurisdiction had it in civil causes?
17. What jurisdiction had the Exchequer?
18. What was the jurisdiction of the Common Pleas?
19. What were the duties and powers, originally, of a Chancellor?
20. How did his equitable jurisdiction arise?
21. What are the Nisi Prius Courts?
22. After trial at nisi prius, what further proceedings took place?
23. How do courts in this country differ from those just described?
24. What is meant by Superior and Inferior Courts?

25. What courts, in England, correspond to our State Supreme Courts and Courts of Appeals?
26. What is the Court of Admiralty and what its jurisdiction?
27. What jurisdiction had the Ecclesiastical Courts?
28. What courts in this country had the same jurisdiction?
29. What is jurisdiction?
30. What is jurisdiction *in personam* and *in rem?*
31. How does a court acquire jurisdiction to act upon the property of non-residents?
32. How is jurisdiction over the person acquired?
33. How jurisdiction *in rem?*
34. What is the effect of judgment against a person not summoned to appear?
35. Suppose the record of a foreign judgment does not show service of process, what is the presumption of law?
36. If the record recites service, can it be contradicted?
37. What is a writ of *procedendo?*
38. What is a writ of prohibition?
39. What is a mandamus?
40. In what cases will it issue and in what not?

BLACKSTONE.

Book III, Chapters VIII and IX.

1. How are actions divided?
2. What is the difference between them?
3. What is the remedy for an injury with force?
4. For those without force?
5. What is assault?
6. What battery?
7. What mayhem?
8. What is the defence of *son assault demesne?*
9. What is the origin of the action of trespass on the case?
10. What kinds of actions are embraced under the general denomination of actions on the case?

11. What is slander?
12. What is necessary to make slander actionable?
13. What imputations are slanderous?
14. What is a *per quod?*
15. What was *scandalum magnatum?*
16. What is slander of title?
17. What are privileged communications?
18. Is the truth a defence in slander?
19. Is probable cause?
20. What is libel?
21. How does it differ from spoken slander?
22. Why are privileged communications excepted from the law of libel?
23. What is malicious prosecution?
24. What is necessary to make it actionable?
25. What is unlawful imprisonment?
26. What is the remedy?
27. In case of injury to wife or children, what is the remedy?
28. How, in case of seduction?
29. Who must sue for injury to wife?
30. Who for loss of her services?
31. How in case of a child?
32. What is the remedy for injuries to personal property in one's possession?
33. What was the original use of the action of replevin?
34. What its present use?
35. What is the process of replevying in case of distress?
36. What if the goods were secreted or carried off?
37. What is the course of pleading?
38. What was the landlord's defence called?
39. What the bailiff's?
40. What judgment is rendered for the plaintiff where he has received his goods, and where not?
41. What for the defendant?
42. What is the mode of proceeding at the present day?
43. What are the pleadings in other cases than distress?
44. What is necessary to enable the plaintiff to sustain this action?

45. What was the action of detinue, and what were its disadvantages?
46. What was the action of trover?
47. What title is necessary to sustain it?
48. What amounts to conversion?
49. Is knowledge of another's title necessary to make a wrongful conversion?
50. What is recovered in trover?
51. In what case does trespass *vi et armis* lie?
52. What possession is sufficient?
53. If property is leased, who must sue?
54. Who, if it is bailed?
55 What is a debt?
56. What was the action of covenant?
57. What is the action of assumpsit?
58. What is the difference between assumpsit and debt?
59. What are implied assumpsits?
60. What is an assumpsit upon a *quantum meruit?*
61. What are the common counts?
62. What the money counts?
63. What is the object of including these counts in suits on notes?
64. In what cases of express contract may plaintiff sue on the implied contract and declare on the common counts?
65. In case of warranty how does plaintiff declare?

BLACKSTONE.

Book III, Chapters X and XI.

1. What is an ouster?
2. What is abatement?
3. Intrusion?
4. Disseisin?
5. What discontinuance?
6. Could the heir in tail enter after ancestor's death in case of discontinuance?

7. Deforcement is what?
8. What was the importance of entry?
9. What was continual claim?
10. Could entry be made in case of deforcement, and if not, why?
11. What was the remedy where there was no right of entry?
12. What must be shown in it?
13. What will defeat it?
14. What superseded the writ of entry?
15. What was the remedy in case of dower?
16. What was disseisin at election?
17. What was the limitation to these possessory remedies?
18. In what cases must a writ of right be resorted to?
19. In a writ of right what must demandant show?
20. What can defendant show in bar?
21. What were formerly the rights of a tenant for years, when ejected, against the disseisor and against a stranger ousting him?
22. What was the device adopted by the courts to make ejectment applicable to freehold estates?
23. What is the still more modern device?
24. What was enacted to prevent collusion between plaintiffs and tenants?
25. On what is the judgment in ejectment final?
26. Does the action of ejectment remedy the loss of mesne profits?
27. How are they to be recovered?
28. In the action for mesne profits, of what authority is the judgment in ejectment?
29. How if the ejectment be brought against the tenant and action for trespass against the landlord?
30. By what time is the action for mesne profits barred?
31. To what kind of property does this action imply?
32. What application of this remedy is made by Statute 4 Geo. II, to the case of landlord and tenant?

BLACKSTONE.

Book III, Chapters XII, XIII, XIV, XVII.

1. What is trespass to real estate?
2. Must lands be inclosed in order to the commission of trespass?
3. What of passage by the public over uninclosed lands?
4. What possession is necessary and sufficient to sustain an action of trespass?
5. What is constructive possession?
6. How if the land be held adversely?
7. How far does actual possession extend?
8. How, if two parties are in possession, each claiming all, under deeds?
9. Is a right of entry sufficient to maintain trespass?
10. Can tenants in common sue co-tenants in trespass?
11. What amount of force is necessary to make trespass?
12. What if animals stray on land?
13. What if one enter rightfully and afterwards commit some excess?
14. What is the form of averment where the trespass continues from day to day?
15. In what cases are entries, while yet forbidden by possessor, not trespasses?
16. How if one enter a tavern and commit disorder?
17. Under the general issue can special authority be given in evidence?
18. What is the defence of *liberum tenementum?*
19. Has intention anything to do with this wrong?
20. What is the remedy by action for nuisance?
21. What is necessary to enable the plaintiff to maintain the action?
22. Is defendant liable for continuance of the nuisance if on the land when he bought it?
23. What is contributory negligence, and what its effect on the right of action?

24. What if the nuisance exists when one builds, *e.g.*, a slaughter-house?
25. What is waste?
26. Has the tenant for life, in reversion or remainder, a right to sue for waste?
27. How, after a lease for years has expired?
28. Was tenant liable, in the old action, for waste of a stranger?
29. What is a petition of right?
30. What were the remedies of the Crown?
31. What are the remedies of the State or United States in this country?
32. In what cases are inquisitions used?
33. What was the writ of *quo warranto*.
34. What was the judgment?
35. What is the modern form of proceeding?

BLACKSTONE.

Book III, Chapters XVIII, XIX, XX, and XXI.

1. What was the original writ?
2. What its form?
3. What is the general nature of a writ?
4. What is a return?
5. What were the two forms of original writs?
6. What is testing?
7. What are pledges of prosecution?
8. What are return days?
9. What essoigns?
10. What is the first process?
11. What were judicial writs?
12. What is the difference between mesne and final process?
13. What followed the summons?
14. In case of forcible injuries, what was the first process?
15. After attachment what followed?

16. What further, in case of forcible wrongs?
17. By what process did the capias become the first step in the proceedings?
18. What was done if defendant was not found in the sheriff's county?
19. What proceedings were necessary in order to proceed to outlawry against the defendant?
20. How was the capias to be executed?
21. What came to be the practice?
22. Who were privileged from arrest?
23. When could civil process be executed?
24. What breaking could an officer do?
25. Upon arrest, what must the prisoner do?
26. What power has his bail over him?
27. Is the sheriff bound to take bail, and what if he does not?
28. What is defendant to do on return day of the writ?
29. What if he fails to appear?
30. What are the plaintiff's rights as to bail bonds?
31. What was bail to the action?
32. What was justifying by bail?
33. What rights had bail to the action for their own protection from loss?
34. What will discharge bail?
35. Could bail be required in an action for unliquidated damages?
36. Or from executor, etc.?
37. What are pleadings?
38. What was their form anciently?
39. What is the declaration?
40. What are counts?
41. What was the relation between the original writ and the declaration?
42. What the effect of variance between the original writ and the declaration?
43. What are local and what transitory actions?
44. What was the value of different counts?
45. What was meant by the conclusion, "and therefore he brings suit?"

46. What if plaintiff fails to file his declaration in the time required by the rules?
47. What is a *retraxit?*
48. What is a discontinuance?
49. What is making defence?
50. What is an imparlance?
51. What steps could be taken between defence and plea?
52. How many kinds of pleas are there?
53. What effect has death on actions for personal injuries?
54. How of actions on contract or for injuries to property?
55. What was required to make a good plea in abatement; a plea of non-joinder, for example?
56. What if the dilatory pleas were sustained?
57. If overruled or demurred to, what?
58. What must be averred in the plea of tender?
59. What effect has payment into court?
60. Can the defendant plead inconsistent defences?
61. What is the general issue, and what are its forms in different actions?
62. What may be shown under the general issue in assumpsit?
63. What, under "*non est factum?*
64. What are pleas in bar?
65. What are examples?
66. What is the defence of limitations?
67. What does the Statute of James enact as to entries?
68. How do courts of equity act in reference to this statute?
69. Does the statute apply to specialties?
70. What presumptions prevail as to them?
71. What is the limitation as to personal actions?
72. What is the plea of estoppel?
73. What is the rule as to singleness?
74. What, as to directness, certainty, etc.?
75. What is a verification?
76. What is confession and avoidance?
77. What a traverse?
78. What are the names of the pleas in their several stages?
79. How far does the right to use several pleas extend?

80. Illustrate the effect in case of suit on bond with condition?
81. What is tending the issue, and what the form?
82. What is the departure in pleading?
83. What a new assignment, and give examples?
84. What was pleading with a protestation?
85. What is the rule as to pleading what amounts to the general issue?
86. What is giving color?
87. What is the *similiter*?
88. What a demurrer, general and special?
89. What is a plea *puis darrein continuance*?

BLACKSTONE.

Book III, Chapters XXII and XXIII.

1. What is trial by record?
2. How is the issue of *nul tiel record* tried?
3. How in this country?
4. What is provided by the Constitution of the United States as to records?
5. What has Congress enacted?
6. What is the effect of the judgment of one State in another?
7. What is trial by inspection?
8. How would the appointment of a public officer be tried in this country?
9. What was wager of law, and in what cases was it allowed?
10. What was trial by the grand assize?
11. What was the first step towards the jury trial?
12. What came to be the practice in the summoning of juries?
13. How many jurors were summoned?
14. How many sat to try a cause, and how were they selected?
15. What was a challenge to the array, and what the grounds of it?
16. What is a challenge to the polls?
17. What are the grounds?

18. What is a principal challenge, and what a challenge to the favor?
19. How is the latter tried?
20. What is a challenge "*propter delictum?*"
21. What are talesmen?
22. By whom are questions of law and fact, respectively, tried?
23. What means the rule, that a fact must be proved by the best evidence?
24. What is secondary evidence?
25. What kind of apparently hearsay evidence is admitted?
26. How is the attendance of a witness obtained?
27. What is a *subpœna duces tecum?*
28. What is the officer's return if the witness is not found?
29. What witnesses are incompetent to testify?
30. What is a bill of exceptions?
31. To what court did the writ of error and the bill of exceptions go?
32. What is a demurrer to evidence?
33. In what other way can mistakes of the court be corrected?
34. How in this country?
35. What was the ancient theory upon which jurors were selected?
36. What is the present?
37. Can jurors act upon the knowledge of one of their number?
38. What is the charge of the court?
39. In what ways may a verdict be rendered?
40. On what grounds may it be set aside?
41. What is a special verdict?
42. What is a verdict subject to an agreed statement?
43. What were the defects in trial by jury, noticed by the commentator?

BLACKSTONE.

Book III, Chapters XXIV, XXV, and XXVI.

1. What is the *postea?*
2. What is done with it?
3. What proceedings may intervene between verdict and judgment?
4. Is the granting a new trial a matter of right or within the discretion of the court.
5. Does an appeal lie from the ruling of the court on it?
6. How must facts alleged as ground for new trial be brought before the court?
7. What was formerly the remedy for an improper verdict?
8. What is arresting the judgment?
9. What are the grounds for it?
10. What is the judgment on arresting the judgment?
11. What is the difference between the case where the whole declaration is bad and the case where one of several counts is good, but the verdict general?
12. What is a *venire facias de novo?*
13. In what case is a defect cured by the verdict?
14. What is a repleader, and when awarded?
15. How many kinds of judgments are there?
16. What is an interlocutory, and what a final one?
17. What is a judgment by default in a case of damages, and what further proceedings is then had?
18. How of judgment on demurrer in a damage case?
19. Is a judgment for defendant ever interlocutory?
20. What is the form of judgment for either party?
21. What was defendant's recourse if dissatisfied with the judgment?
22. How is relief given in this country in similar cases?
23. What is the office of the writ of error?
24. What errors may be corrected by it?

25. What amendments may be made, and at what time under existing law?
26. What amendments may be made after judgment?
27. Does the writ of error suspend or supersede execution on the judgment?
28. What is the proceeding with an inferior court?
29. What were the various writs of execution called in real actions, ejectment, replevin, debt, trespass, or case?
30. What was the writ of *capias ad satisfaciendum?*
31. What was the sheriff's duty under it?
32. How if he allowed defendant to go at large?
33. In such case, could he retake him?
34. How if the escape was involuntary?
35. What was the effect of taking the defendant under this writ on the judgment
36. If the sheriff returned "*non est inventus*" to this writ, what was the plaintiff's remedy?
37. What was the form of proceeding against bail?
38. What were the writs against the property?
39. What was seized under the writ of *fi. fa.?*

BLACKSTONE.

Book III, Chapter XXVIII.

1. What was the principal origin of equity jurisprudence?
2. Is the court of equity less bound by statutes than the common law courts?
3. What is the difference in their remedies in the case of a contract for the sale of land?
4. How, in case of a contract procured by fraud?
5. What is meant by equity following the law?
6. How of the maxims: "When equities are equal, the law prevails;" "He who seeks equity must do equity;" "Equity delights in equality;" and "Equity will consider that as done which was agreed to be done."

7. Give examples of equity relief in case of accidental loss?
8. In case of defective execution of power?
9. In whose favor is relief given in this case?
10. What difference between mistakes of fact and law?
11. Into what two classes do frauds distribute themselves?
12. What sort of misrepresentation or concealment will amount to fraud?
13. What is constructive fraud?
14. What jurisdiction does a court of equity exercise in matters of account, dower, and partition?
15. How, as to specific performance of personal contracts?
16. Contracts for sale of land?
17. When not in writing?
18. Injunctions?
19. Mortgages?
20. What is the form of commencing a suit in equity?
21. How is answer enforced?
23. How is testimony taken?
23. What is an interlocutory, and what a final decree?
24. What are issues?

BLACKSTONE.

Book IV, Chapters I to XIV.

1. What is a crime?
2. What is essential to make a crime?
3. Who are incapable of crimes?
4. At what age is a child *doli capax?*
5. Can an infant under fourteen be convicted of rape?
6. As accessory?
7. In what cases will insane delusion be a defence, and in what not?
8. How, if the crime be not connected with the delusion?
9. What effect has drunkenness on the party's responsibility?
10. How does it affect the question of intent?

11. How does mistake of law or fact affect the question of guilt?
12. In what case will compulsion excuse?
13. To what offences does the rule apply?
14. Can a wife be convicted as accessory to husband?
15. Can husband and wife be convicted of conspiracy?
16. What are principals, and what accessories?
17. In how many degrees may one be principal?
18. What constitutes presence to make one a principal?
19. Will presence, without actual participation, make one a principal?
20. How can one be principal in another's suicide?
21. What are seconds in a duel?
22. How if one be merely travelling to the place of action?
23. In what cases of crime was there no distinction between principals and accessories?
24. To what extent is the accessory before the fact responsible for the principal's act?
25. What acts make one accessory after the fact?
26. Would concealment by wife make her accessory?
27. Is a receiver of stolen goods an accessory?
28. How far must the felony be complete to make one accessory?
29. How was accessory to be punished at common law?
30. On trial of an accessory, what weight has the record of the principal's conviction?
31. Can one acquitted as principal, be convicted as accessory?
32. What are the common law offences against the law of nations?
33. What is piracy?
34. What was petit treason at common law?
35. What the principal high treason as defined by statute?
36. Do words or intentions ever amount to treason?
37. What is treason against the United States?
38. Is a *conspiracy* to levy war against the United States treason?
39. What is adhering to the enemies, etc.?
40. How must treason be proved?
41. What were felonies?
42. What are considered felonies in this country?
43. What was *præmunire?*

44. What misprisions?
45. What was barratry? Maintenance? Champerty?
46. What was perjury?
47. What will amount to it?
48. Under what circumstances must the oath be administered?
49. In what kind of court?
50. Must it be in a cause pending?
51. How material must the fact be?
52. What is subornation of perjury?
53. What is an affray?
54. What an unlawful assembly?
55. Rout? Riot?
56. What is necessary to make a riot?
57. How of persons present at a riot and not aiding to suppress it?
58. How of a frolic carried on with alarming demonstrations?
59. What is forcible entry and detainer?
60. What amounts to a forcible entry and what not?
61. What is libel?
62. How does the criminal differ from the civil law of libel?
63. Is the truth a defence to an indictment?
64. What is *scandalum magnatum?*
65. What are privileged communications?
66. What are the functions of the jury in case of libel?
67. What is usury? What is cheating?
68. What false pretences?
69. Forestalling? Regrating? Engrossing?
70. What kind of false pretence is criminal?
71. Is the representation of a future act, to be done?
72. A nuisance is what?

BLACKSTONE.

Book IV, Chapters XIV to XVIII.

1. How many kinds of homicide are there?
2. What is justifiable?

3. What if a judge, without lawful commission, condemns to death, or an officer executes?
4. How if the place, time, or form of death is varied?
5. What justifies homicide by permission?
6. Will prevention of crimes not accompanied with force justify homicide?
7. What is the difference between justification and excuse?
8. Excusable homicide is what?
9. What if a person be engaged in an unlawful act?
10. Or a dangerous act?
11. How of self-defence?
12. What is the difference between killing in self-defence and manslaughter?
13. What does the law require a party to do in case of deadly assault?
14. How in a duel if one retreat and then kill?
15. In whose defence may one kill another?
16. Can one kill in defence of his property from mere trespass?
17. In case of excusable homicide what is the punishment?
18. What is manslaughter?
19. What provocation will reduce homicide from murder to manslaughter?
20. How as to the proportion between the provocation and the resentment?
21. How if one find a mere trespasser on his lands and beat his brains out?
22. If words lead to a fight and one is killed in the heat of it, what is it?
23. How if the provocation was a mere excuse for gratifying an old enmity?
24. What are cases of involuntary manslaughter?
25. How does the character of the act being done affect the accidental killing?
26. If A strikes B's horse so that he runs over and kills a child, what is it?
27. How of an accidental homicide by one of several conspiring to commit felony?

28. How if he turn aside to commit felony foreign to the common purpose?
29. What of death resulting from carelessness; *e.g.*, throwing down a brick from a house?
30. How of undue correction of child or apprentice?
31. How of malpractice by a physician?
32. How is manslaughter treated as to punishment?
33. What is murder?
34. Who are incapable of committing it?
35. Can an unborn child be murdered?
36. What is the rule about the *corpus delicti?*
37. Within what time must death follow an injury to make it murder; why?
38. What is the difference between malice expressed and implied?
39. In what cases will malice be implied when the killing is upon sudden provocation?
40. How if one attempts to kill one and accidentally kills another?
41. How if a man drive recklessly into a crowd or let loose a ferocious beast, etc.?
42. What was petit treason at common law?
43. What is mayhem?
44. How far is intention necessary?
45. What if one knock out a fore tooth accidentally in the heat of a fight?
46. Can husband be guilty of rape upon his wife? Of being accessory to rape by another?
47. At what age could a female consent to carnal connection so that it would not be rape?
48. What constitutes force; and is it rape if submission is secured by threats of death?
49. How if a woman is deceived into the belief that the man is her husband or that she is undergoing medical treatment?
50. How if the woman be drugged?
51. Can a prostitute be the subject of rape?

52. Would her character be properly in evidence on an indictment for rape?
53. How does intent to kill or ravish affect the criminal character of an assault?
54. What was arson?
55. How much burning is necessary?
56. Will negligent setting on fire amount to arson?
57. Will burning one's own house be arson?
58. How if under lease?
59. What kind of house is subject to arson?
60. What is burglary?
61. What house is the subject of it?
62. How with the room of a college student or boarder?
63. How of a town-house of a corporation?
64. What is a sufficient breaking?
65. Is entry through open door or window?
66. Is breaking a pane of glass and putting the hand in and stealing something?
67. Opening with a skeleton key?
68. How if, being inside by stealth, the thief unlocks an inside door?
69. How of entry by trick, false pretence, or show of authority, followed up by a felonious attempt to rob?
70. How of entry through conspiracy with a servant?
71. Would this be the burglary by both?
72. What must be the intent?
73. What is averred in the indictment for burglary?
74. What is larceny, simple and compound?
75. What are the essential elements?
76. What taking is necessary?
77. In what cases may one, already in possession, take feloniously?
78. On what principle?
79. How of a bale opened by a carrier?
80. How of goods obtained by fraud with intent to steal?
81. How, if the original taking was innocent, and the party changed his mind and determined to convert?

82. Can a man steal his own goods, and when?
83. Can a wife steal her husband's goods?
84. What kind of removal is sufficient to make a taking?
85. What intent is necessary?
86. How, if a horse is taken and let loose?
87. What is the subject of larceny; are bonds, bills, etc.?
88. How as to ownership?
89. What is robbery?
90. What amounts to putting in fear?
91. Is furtive taking and forcible holding robbery?
92. What is the punishment?
93. What is forgery?
94. What uttering?

BLACKSTONE.

Book IV, Chapter XVIII to end.

1. What is a recognizance?
2. What its object?
3. What was done with it on breach?
4. How is it forfeited?
5. How discharged?
6. What courts have criminal jurisdiction?
7. What jurisdiction had the House of Peers and Court of the Lord High Steward?
8. What corresponds with it in this country?
9. What was the jurisdiction of the King's Bench and Courts of Nisi Prius?
10. How were offences inquired into in these courts?
11. What are summary proceedings?
12. What restraints are imposed on the inferior courts?
13. What must appear in their proceedings?
14. In what case will writ of *certiorari* issue and at what stage of the proceedings below?
15. How are contempts dealt with?

16. What are contempts?
17. Who is to judge of the fact of contempt?
18. What is the limit to the judge's power?
19. What is a warrant and by whom issued?
20. On what evidence does a justice issue his warrant?
21. What is its form?
22. How must the accused be described?
23. Will a warrant wholly illegal in form, justify an officer who arrests?
24. How of a regular warrant?
25. At what time and place may criminal warrants be executed?
26. When may an officer arrest without warrant?
27. When the sheriff or coroner?
28. How, if an officer arrest without warrant or information?
29. What may be done by an officer in attempting to arrest a felon?
30. When may a private person make an arrest?
31. What may he do in making the arrest?
32. What may a private person do to prevent a felony?
33. What is to be done on arrest?
34. How is the accused to be examined?
35. In what cases is bail admitted?
36. What of excessive bail?
37. What is the commitment?
38. What is an indictment, and what a presentment?
39. What effect had the inquest of a coroner's jury at common law?
40. How in this country?
41. What is a grand jury?
42. What is their action?
43. What rules govern as to the form of the indictment?
44. What are informations?
45. What was an appeal?
46. What was outlawry, and what the effect of a judgment of outlawry?
47. What is the arraignment?

48. Could the accessory be arraigned before the principal's conviction?
49. When may he be tried?
50. What was standing mute, and what the consequence?
51. What are the general pleadings to indictments?
52. What judgment is given if a demurrer is overruled?
53. Can a motion in arrest be made?
54. What are the usual pleas in bar?
55. What is the effect of a former conviction or acquittal of the same offence?
56. What if the former proceedings resulted in a disagreement and discharge of the jury or the judgment was arrested?
57. What was the effect of a former attainder for another offence?
58. How is a pardon pleaded?
59. If a special plea be found against the prisoner or had on demurrer, what then?
60. What right of challenge had the prisoner?
61. How if he challenged more than 35?
62. In what cases are more than one witness necessary to convict?
63. Can the jury render a privy verdict as in civil cases?
64. May they render a special verdict?
65. How far will a court interfere with a verdict?
66. On conviction of larceny, what rights enured to the prosecutor?
67. At common law, what were his rights as to the stolen goods?
68. What was the benefit of clergy?
69. What is the result of legislation on this subject?
70. Upon the verdict of guilty, what next in felonies and misdemeanors?
71. Are errors cured by verdict as in civil cases?
72. On what ground can the judgment be arrested?
73. What was the effect of judgment of death?
74. What the difference between mere conviction and attainder?
75. What forfeiture resulted?
76. How far back does it go?
77. How if a party die before judgment or is killed in open rebellion?

78. What difference between the lands and the goods?
79. Was a writ of error necessary when a court had not jurisdiction?
80. What of execution in such cases?
81. How far was a purchaser from a prisoner bound by his conviction?
82. Reprieve and pardon are what?
83. In what cases and by whom were prisoners reprieved?
84. To what extent could the king pardon?
85. May the pardon be conditional?
86. How soon must it be pleaded?
87. What effect has attainder?
88. Do the time and place of the execution form part of the judgment?
89. Could the punishment prescribed be changed?

—

PARSONS ON CONTRACTS.

JOINT CONTRACTS.

Book I, Chapters 1, 2.

1. What is a contract?
2. An obligation?
3. A parol contract?
4. What is a joint contract?
5. What a joint and several?
6. Can a contract be joint and several as to the obligees?
7. What is the difference between the rights and liabilities under a joint contract?
8. Can a party treat the contract as joint in reference to some but not all of the promisors?
9. How must he sue on joint and several contracts?
10. Where two promise, is it presumed joint or several?
11. What has the question of interest in the subject to do with the construction?

12. Where, on lease by several tenants in common, tenants covenanted to pay separate rents to each, was it held joint to the lessors, or several?
13. How if the several interests of the promisees grow out of the contract itself and did not exist before?
14. How of a promise to several to pay an annuity to one?
15. If that one died, what?
16. If the promise is to pay to several, is it several, because their respective interests are designated?
17. How of covenants implied by law, as on a lease by several tenants in common?
18. If several loan money in separate sums to one, how is his promise construed in case of doubt?
19. If a gross sum made up by subscriptions be loaned by several, how?
20. Can a purely joint contract be severed by consent?
21. How does a release by one of several joint obligees affect the joint debt?
22. How of a release by creditors to one of several joint debtors?
23. How of a release to one of several joint and several debtors?
24. If a formal release under seal be given to one of several debtors, and the other promises to remain bound, what effect has it?
25. What is the difference between a release and a covenant not to sue?
26. What between a general covenant not to sue a single debtor and one not to sue one of several debtors?
27. What is the effect of a release to one with reservation of right to sue the other?
28. How is releasor to sue the others in such case?
29. What is the effect of a discharge in bankruptcy of one of several, as a release?
30. How, if procured at the creditor's instance?
31. What of an accord and satisfaction with one, and how far must it go?
32. How of a release, in this respect?

33. What was the effect of death of one of several joint obligors?
34. Of all except one?
35. Is there any right of action against the executors of the deceased?
36. Has the survivor any right of contribution against the deceased's estate?
37. How, if survivor was surety and deceased principal?
38. What is the effect of death where the contract is joint and several?
39. How of death of one of several obligees?
40. How of distribution after recovery?
41. What is the creditor's remedy against joint debtors after judgment?
42. What against joint and several debtors?
43. What is the effect of judgment on a joint note?
44. How on a joint and several note?
45. What is the best way to sue on a joint and several note?
46. How are the expressed and implied obligations of joint trustees, executors, etc., treated?
47. What rights has one of several debtors compelled to pay the whole?
48. Is there any difference whether the co-contractors are principals or sureties?
49. Must the payment be compulsory to entitle to an action for contribution?
50. If one of several sureties dies, can the survivor who pays the debt, even in equity, compel contribution?
51. What contribution can be required at law?
52. In equity?
53. What of collaterals that one surety may have?
54. Is the obligation of several sureties to contribute to one who has paid in full, joint or several?
55. What effect would a release to one have on the obligation of the others?
56. From what time does this obligation of contribution date?
57. If one surety is discharged as to the creditor, does that discharge the contract of contribution?

58. Is there any duty of contribution in case of successive indorsers?
59. How if they are all accommodation parties?
60. Can one of joint makers of a note revive a debt barred by limitations?
61. How of joint and several makers?
62. What is the contract of partnership, joint or joint and several?

PARSONS ON CONTRACTS.

AGENCY.

Book I, Chapters 3, 4.

1. Who are capable of appointing agents, and who incapable?
2. Who may act as agents?
3. Can one be agent and principal also?
4. Can one discharge duties which involve personal trust by another?
5. Can an agent act by an agent?
6. What exceptions?
7. What is the difference between general and special agent?
8. Of what importance is the distinction?
9. How far is a third person dealing with the agent affected by private instructions?
10. What is an attorney in fact?
11. How can an agent be authorized to execute sealed instruments?
12. How to execute simple contracts?
13. How, if they are within the Statute of Frauds?
14. What effect has a ratification of agent's acts?
15. How if he make a contract within the Statute of Frauds?
16. Can a deed, made in the principal's name, be ratified by parol?
17. How, if the agent acts in his own name, can his acts be made those of another by ratification?

18. What exceptions are there to the effect of a ratification? Examples.
19. What as to tenants?
20. Commercial paper?
21. Conversion from demand and refusal?
22. Can the principal ratify so as to acquire rights?
23. How if he ratify an insurance after loss?
24. In what cases can a contract by deed be ratified by parol?
25. Can principal ratify sub-agent's acts?
26. Can agent do so?
27. What is the effect of ratification?
28. How must agent execute a deed for his principal?
29. How if he signs his own name with a seal?
30. What the effect of so executing a lease in the principal's name?
31. How as to informal contracts by parol?
32. If no principal is named, is the agent bound when the principal is discovered?
33. Is the latter?
34. How can he be sued on a written contract if not named?
35. Does an authority to collect debts include an authority to submit to arbitration?
36. Can one authorized to sell, sell on credit?
37. Can an agent pledge his principal's goods?
38. Can an agent, supplied with acceptances in blank, bind his principal by a transfer of them?
39. When a contract is made by an agent, who can sue on it, as to deeds and other written instruments?
40. Can a principal sue on a contract to which he is not a party?
41. What exceptions are there?
42. How in ordinary verbal transactions, as sales or purchases by an agent?
43. How if the agent, meanwhile, has settled with the principal or a third person?
44. Can the principal cut out the agent's lien on the debt for his commission?
45. Or defeat any set-off between the agent and the third person?

46. In what cases is the agent liable to third persons on a contract?
47. How if in the instrument unauthorized there are no words to charge him?
48. If it is a deed in name of the principal?
49. How if there is no responsible principal?
50. How of agents for voluntary associations, clubs, etc.?
51. What has the fact of giving exclusive credit to one or the other to do with it?
52. What is the rule as to revocation of agency?
53. What effect has death?
54. What notice is necessary to third persons?
55. How, when an agency is partly executed?
56. How, of an authority coupled with an interest?
57. How if given for value?
58. What kind of interest must it be?
59. In case of value given for it, what is the difference between revocation by act of law and by act of party?
60. What is the effect of an agent's death?
61. For what acts of the agent is the principal responsible?
62. How does notice to the agent affect the principal?
63. Can an agent set up a stranger's title?
64. Can he buy his principal's property?
65. How, if he mixes his principal's property with his own?
66. What difference is there between public and private agents?
67. What, between factors and brokers?
68. What is a *del credere* agent?
69. Is the agent principal debtor or merely guarantor?
70. What can the factor do with his principal's goods?
71. What rights has he as against his principal?
72. Has a broker any lien?
73. Can either be agent of both parties?

PARSONS ON CONTRACTS.

Book I, Chapter 12.

1. What is a partnership?
2. What is the difference between partnership *inter sese* and as to third persons?
3. In what may the partnership exist?
4. Is there a partnership in real estate at common law?
5. Where one partner dies, is his interest in the real estate of the firm to be considered real or personal as to his heirs or widow?
6. What is the good-will of a partnership?
7. How far will the courts recognize it?
8. How of a professional partnership?
9. Can the membership of a partnership be changed without the consent of all?
10. What is the effect of an assignment, by one, of all his interest?
11. How of an assignment, by all, for the benefit of creditors; do the assignees become partners?
12. Will an action lie on an agreement to become partners?
13. Will a Court of Equity specifically enforce it?
14. Where for a term certain?
15. What effect has a sharing of profits only between parties *inter sese?*
16. How if a part of the profits are set aside to pay creditors, do the latter become partners?
17. How if two firms, engaged in distinct trades, agree to divide losses and profits?
18. What is the effect of sharing profits only?
19. What of a loan to a firm for interest and a share in the profits?
20. In what case will a sharing of profits not make one partner as to third persons?
21. Does joint ownership make a partnership?
22. What beyond that is necessary?

23. What right of suit exists between partners?
24. If one collects money can the other sue at law for a share of it?
25. Can one sue the other on special contracts relating to the business of the firm?
26. If one is a member of two firms, how can one sue the other?
27. What are dormant partners?
28. On what contracts of the firm are they responsible?
29. Is it necessary for them to sue and be sued?
30. On what contracts would they be suable, made after their separation from the firm?
31. Who may dissolve the partnership as to third persons?
32. How does a contract to continue for a certain time affect the right?
33. What notice is necessary?
34. How if there was no notice, as to one who never knew the dormant partner was a member?
35. How far is he bound on old contracts?
36. How is he discharged from them?
37. How if a creditor continue an account current with the new or remaining members?
38. What is a nominal partner?
39. What are his liabilities?
40. When does the partnership begin when several purchase property for joint use in business?
41. How far can one partner bind the firm?
42. By admissions?
43. What limit is there to the power?
44. How about borrowing money in the firm name and afterwards misapplying it?
45. Can one sell or assign the whole partnership property?
46. Does money borrowed in a private name and used for partnership purposes become a partnership debt?
47. Can one partner bind the other by contracts as to realty?
48. Can a stranger take partnership paper for individual debts?
49. Can one generally give a guaranty in the name of the firm?
50. How as to releases, notices, etc., to and by one of the firm?

51. Can one bind the others by deed?
52. In what case may he do so?
53. How of a parol authority or ratification?
54. How of releases?
55. How if the sealed instrument would be valid without seal?
56. How of confessing a judgment against the firm?
57. Is the one executing, etc., in these cases bound?
58. Does a majority control?
59. How does dissolution take place?
60. Can one dissolve at pleasure a partnership for a term certain?
61. What is the effect of an assignment by one partner?
62. What is the effect of the death of one?
63. How of insanity, imprisonment for life, etc.?
64. Bankruptcy?
65. Can executor carry on a partnership business, and what is his liability?
66. On death of one what becomes of the assets?
67. What are the rights of the administrators of deceased?
68. What remedy has a creditor of a firm?
69. What the creditors of one partner?
70. What does he acquire by levy and purchase?
71. How are the assets administered in case of insolvency, or in equity?
72. While partnership is in existence can joint creditors assert any lien or prevent distribution among partners?
73. What are limited partnerships?

PARSONS ON CONTRACTS.

Book I, Chapters 13, 14.

1. What is a novation?
2. What is essential to it?
3. What is the rule in equity about assignment of debts?
4. What assignment does a court of law recognize?
5. How of a check drawn on a bank?

6. What equities would an assignment of a debt be subject to?
7. What effect has the assignment of a debt upon the securities?
8. What amounts to an equitable assignment of a fund?
9. If, after assignment, the debtor should pay the assignor, what remedy would assignee have?
10. How are covenants of title assigned?
11. What covenants pass by a transfer of title?

PARSONS ON CONTRACTS.

Book II, Chapters 1, 2.

1. What is a consideration?
2. Does a deed require a consideration?
3. What will be a sufficient consideration?
4. What is a gift?
5. Is a moral consideration sufficient?
6. How of a promise by a widow to pay for necessaries bought during coverture?
7. How if goods are furnished on the faith of her separate estate and a subsequent promise is made?
8. What is required as to the adequacy of the consideration?
9. How in the case of foolish bargains, and extravagant undertakings for small consideration?
10. How if a promise is founded on an obligation erroneously assumed to exist?
11. How of a promise to one in consideration of his doing something which he is already bound to do?
12. Is the settlement and compromise of doubtful claims a valuable consideration?
13. Dismissal of a suit? Forbearance? How if the claim is ill-founded?
14. Need the promisor be interested in the suit?
15. What inconvenience to promisee is sufficient?
16. Is a legal obligation sufficient without new consideration?

17. Is an assignment which could only be enforced in equity sufficient?
18. Will a past consideration, as work or service rendered gratuitously, suffice?
19. In what case?
20. Is there any difference between not doing and misdoing as to gratuitous promises?
21. What is an executory consideration, and what is sufficient?
22. What is mutuality and the effect of its absence?
23. How if I promise to pay money if another will furnish goods to a third person?
24. How if I revoke the promise?
25. What exceptions to the general rule of mutuality are there?
26. How of subscriptions to stock, is there mutuality?
27. How if expenses are incurred on the faith of the subscriptions?
28. How of subscriptions under seal?
29. How if one of several considerations is frivolous or is insufficient, as in consideration of the forbearance of a good debt and a bad one?
30. How if part of the consideration is illegal?
31. How if the consideration is good but part of the promises illegal?
32. How if there is a legal promise on one side and on the other several, of which one is illegal?
33. What of an impossible consideration?
34. What kind of impossibility must it be?
35. How of a promise to do what is beyond the pecuniary means only of the promisor?
36. How if the consideration was possible at the time the contract was made, but became impossible afterwards?
37. What is a failure of consideration?
38. What is the effect of a total failure?
39. What is the effect of a partial failure?
40. When divisible? When not?
41. How take advantage of a partial failure in the latter case?

42. How if the work is so defective as to be useless to the party retaining it?
43. If not useless but short of the contract?'
44. How of partial failure as to promissory notes?
45. How if the money has been paid, and the consideration fails afterwards?
46. If the promise to pay one person on consideration received from another, who can sue?
47. How as to money simply paid to one for another?
48. How if the agreement is in writing or under seal?
49. If money is loaned to another and I afterwards guarantee its repayment, is the consideration sufficient to sustain my promise?
50. How if loaned at my request?
51. In what cases will a previous request be implied by law?
52. How if I voluntarily pay a judgment against another and he afterwards promises to repay me?
53. How if I retain the consideration?
54. How if one send me household supplies which I consume and promise to pay for?
55. How if a man repairs my house in my absence?
56. What kind of assent is necessary to complete a contract?
57. How if a proposition is accepted with conditions?
58. How if assent is called for in a certain form, as in writing, and given otherwise?
59. How if one gives a letter of credit guaranteeing advances on certain terms, will it cover any made on different terms?
60. How long can an offer be withdrawn?
61. What is an auction sale in regard to offer and acceptance?
62. How soon must an offer be accepted ordinarily?
63. How of giving one the refusal of property?
64. How if a person paid for it?
65. Where an offer is made by mail, when is its acceptance complete?
66. Up to what time and how may it be recalled?
67. Is silence acceptance?

PARSONS ON CONTRACTS.

Book III, Chapters 2 and 3, to Sec. 7 inclusive.

1. What is the nature of an auction sale?
2. What bearing have printed terms and conditions on it?
3. What is the effect of errors of description?
4. How of a condition that this shall not affect the sale, but that allowances shall be made?
5. If there is no such condition, can the seller insist on the sale with allowances for material errors?
6. If lots are sold at a distinct price for each, how does failure of title as to some affect the sale?
7. How if a gross price is paid for the whole?
8. How is a sale affected by the employment of puffers or by-bidders?
9. How of reserving a bid to prevent sacrifice?
10. How if the sale is announced to be without reserve?
11. Whose agent is the auctioneer?
12. As to signing the memorandum of sale?
13. After sale properly noted, can he interfere with it, release either party, etc.?
14. When does he become personally responsible?
15. Can he purchase, himself?
16. If the vendor cannot make a good title what can the buyer do?
17. How if purchaser has given notes and received no deed and the title cannot be made?
18. At what time must the vendor have a good title?
19. If a purchaser does not demand a good title and rescind and the seller sues for price, what must he show as to title?
20. How is time regarded in equity?
21. If the title turns out defective, what as to purchaser's deposit with the auctioneer?
22. Can he sue for damages for loss of his bargain?
23. What is an exception to this rule?

24. If the title turns out bad after the deed has passed what redress has the purchaser?
25. If he is sued on notes given, what?
26. What must plaintiff do before suing on a contract for sale of real estate?

---

27. What is a sale of a chattel?
28. When does the title pass?
29. How if the price be not paid immediately, or payment is waived?
30. When does the right of possession pass?
31. What title must one have to make a sale?
32. What difference is there between selling goods stolen and those acquired through a fraudulent contract?
33. Can one sell what is not yet in existence?
34. What would such a contract be?
35. How, of a contract to deliver articles yet to be manufactured?
36. What is potential existence?
37. If one contracts to sell what does not exist, and afterwards acquires it, does title pass without a new sale?
38. Does a contract to manufacture goods pass title when they are manufactured?
39. How, if the subject of sale is partially destroyed?
40. How, in case of specific articles of which some are totally lost?
41. How in case all are partially destroyed?
42. What certainty is requisite as to price?
43. What is a waiver of seller's lien for price?
44. How if the article remain in possession until the note matures?
45. At whose risk are the goods when the sale is complete but the price not paid?
46. When is the sale complete so as to pass the title?
47. How if one buys so many bushels yet to be measured?
48. How if several own in common, can one transfer so many bushels by order on the warehouseman, accepted, without being measured off?

49. If articles being manufactured are lost, who bears the loss?
50. Is there any difference if the delay is the buyer's fault?
51. If part payment is made in advance?
52. How if the quantity of goods to be taken is yet to be ascertained?
53. How if the price is only to be ascertained by measurement at a certain rate per foot, but the property is identified?
54. What effect as to third persons has the retaining possession by the vendor?
55. How may delivery be made?
56. How of symbolical delivery?
57. How if the property is left on the seller's premises, but to be under the control of the buyer?
58. Where must the seller deliver?
59. If seller assumes to deliver elsewhere than at home, at what time must it be?
60. If the seller fails to deliver according to agreement, who is responsible for the goods?
61. How if the buyer refuse to receive them?
62. If buyer refuses compliance with the conditions of sale and seller sues for the price, what must and can he do with the goods?
63. What is the effect of the sale in such a case?
64. If goods are sold on credit and buyer becomes insolvent before delivery, what is the seller's right?
65. Where must a note payable in goods be paid?
66. What is the difference between tender of money and goods in payment?
67. What of conditional sales as to passing of title, and what is the seller's remedy for non-payment?
68. How if goods are sold with option of returning within a certain time?
69. What is the practice of brokers as to memoranda of sale?
70. Which is the real contract, the broker's book or the bought and sold notes?
71. How, if there are no notes?
72. How if one note differs from the book and the other not?

73. How if the subject-matter is differently described in the two notes, even by mistake?
74. What is sufficient evidence in an action on such a sale?
75. Can parol evidence be received to add to them?
76. What if the broker does not disclose his principal?
77. Can he sign for either party after sale is made?
78. Can a factor pass bought and sold notes?

PARSONS ON CONTRACTS.

Chapters 4, 5 and 6.

1. What is a sale "to arrive?"
2. Is such a sale a mere agreement to sell or an executed sale?
3. How if the sale is by a bill of lading?
4. Is such a sale a warranty that the vessel will arrive?
5. Or is it a sale on condition that it shall arrive?
6. Does it ordinarily pass property in any specific chattel?
7. Is it a warranty that the goods will arrive if the vessel does?
8. If the vessel and goods arrive but consigned to another, is the seller still bound?
9. How of a sale of goods at sea?
10. How of a sale of goods to arrive before a day certain?
11. How of a sale of goods to be shipped on a certain vessel?
12. How does a sale "to arrive" differ from a sale of goods at sea, with delivery of bill of lading, etc.?
13. How if the goods are destroyed or sold?
14. What difference is there between a mortgage of chattels and realty?
15. Can a mortgage be made to cover future-acquired property?
16. How as to mortgage of a stock of goods retained and retailed by the mortgagor?
17. What is the effect generally of retention of possession by mortgagor?
18. What implied warranty is there on a sale of chattels?
19. How does the want of possession affect it?

20. How as to quality?
21. What amounts to warranty, though not such in form?
22. In what excepted cases is there implied warranty?
23. How when purchaser has no opportunity to inspect the goods?
24. How when manufactured goods are ordered for a particular purpose?
25. How if the object of the purchase is known, but the thing is not expressly ordered for that?
26. What warranty is there on a sale by sample?
27. What if there is a secret defect in the sample?
28. How as to sales of household provisions?
29. Does an express warranty extend to patent defects?
30. How as to soundness, when delivered in future?
31. What is the remedy if goods warranted be accepted and afterwards are discovered to be defective?
32. Must the buyer return goods before suing on the warranty?
33. May he return them and sue for their price?
34. How if part have been sold?
35. How if the seller refuse to receive back the goods?
36. In an action for the price, may the breach of warranty be shown?
37. What would the damages be if the goods are returned?
38. What, if not returned?
39. Is there any warranty on judicial sales?
40. What is the right of stoppage *in transitu?*
41. What amounts to insolvency in the sense of this rule?
42. Does the mere insolvency in itself arrest the goods and destroy the buyer's right to them?
43. Is an actual seizure necessary?
44. What kind of notice will suffice?
45. When must the insolvency take place to justify the stoppage?
46. Is this right a mere extension of the seller's lien, or is it a right of rescission?
47. Can a bailee having a mere lien exercise this right?
48. Does it exist as to money remitted, and that without reference to the state of the accounts between the parties?

49. How if the consignor has received a bill of exchange for the goods or been partly paid?
50. How if the goods are consigned in payment of an existing debt?
51. How long may this right be exercised?
52. What if the goods are delivered to a carrier named by the consignee?
53. What if in a warehouse on the route, or in the custom-house waiting the payment of duties?
54. How if carried to the vendee's wharf but possession not yet taken by him?
55. How if shipped in a vessel of the consignee, but by the bill of lading they are to be delivered to the consignor?
56. What kind of delivery to consignee will suffice to terminate the transit?
57. How if the goods are shipped for another market, and not to go into consignee's hands?
58. How is the right of stoppage destroyed?
59. What is the form of a bill of lading?
60. What is the effect of a transfer or indorsement of a bill of lading?
61. Will delivery without endorsement of the bill, or *vice versa*, pass title to the goods?
62. How if the bill of lading is pledged?
63. Is the right affected by an attachment by the vendee's creditor or the carrier's lien?
64. If the creditor reserve a right of property by the bill of lading until payment, would the assignment of bill defeat the right of stoppage?
65. What of an agreement by a debtor, on the eve of insolvency, to return goods to seller?

PARSONS ON CONTRACTS.

BOOK III, CHAPTER 7, and SECS. 1 TO 4 OF CHAPTER 11.

1. What is a guaranty?
2. What is the obligation of the guarantor said to be?
3. Can there be a guarantor without a principal who is bound?
4. What is the difference between promising to pay for goods furnished by another and promising to see them paid for?
5. What will be a sufficient consideration for the guaranty if simultaneous with the debt?
6. If after the debt?
7. What would be the effect of any fraud or concealment on the surety's obligation?
8. What difference is there between the delivery of debtor's property to him on promise by another to see the debt paid, and delivering it to the new promisor himself?
9. What is the effect of charging on the seller's books to the new promisor or the debtor?
10. What acceptance is necessary to complete the contract of guaranty?
11. What is a continuing letter of credit?
12. What is the duty of the party furnishing goods, as to this?
13. How if the contract of the principal is changed after the guaranty is given?
14. What change would discharge the guarantor?
15. Does a guaranty of the obligation of two extend to the acts of one?
16. Or a guaranty to several bind in favor of the survivors?
17. Does a guaranty to a partnership extend to the survivors?
18. Would a guaranty of good conduct of an employé be considered good in favor of obligee's executors?
19. How will a guaranty of payment for goods of a certain amount be considered?
20. What acceptance or notice is necessary in such cases?
21. What will discharge the guarantor?

22. What is the effect of giving time to the principal debtor?
23. How of a covenant not to sue the principal?
24. How of a covenant not to sue for a limited time?
25. How of such a covenant reserving the right to sue the surety?
26. How of forbearance to sue the principal?
27. How of forbearance when surety demands that principal shall be sued?
28. How as to collaterals in creditor's hands?
29. Would receiving interest in advance on an overdue note discharge the surety?
30. How if time be given to several promisors when one only, as between themselves, was surety?
31. How if the creditor knew this?
32. Is notice of default to guarantors necessary?
33. What notice to guarantors of promissory notes?
34. What is the liability on a guaranty of the collection of a debt?
35. What rights has guarantor on payment of the debt?
36. What as to collaterals?
37. Under what circumstances can a guaranty be revoked?
38. In case of a continuing letter of credit?
39. How, if for a consideration?
40. How, if it is a guaranty of good conduct in an office or employment?

PARSONS ON CONTRACTS.

Book III, Chapter 11.

1. What is a bailment?
2. What are the three general classes?
3. What degree of care is required in each?
4. How far does the old rule of diligence apply to common carriers?
5. What is the test of the bailee's diligence, such as he exercises in his own affairs, or such as people ordinarily use?
6. What of increase and deterioration when the bailment is returned to the bailor?

7. What of claims by strangers on the property?
8. How if the whole is claimed by each of two or more bailors?
9. What kind of interest has the gratuitous bailee and what actions may he bring?
10. Are deposits in bank bailments?
11. What is the pledgee when his debt is paid?
12. What the finder of chattels?
13. Is the finder of a note entitled to collect it?
14. Could the maker pay him, knowing his want of title?
15. Has a mandatary any special property?
16. What is a bank as to notes left for collection by its customers, without charge?
17. How far are they liable for neglects of notaries, other agents, and banks?
18. When the undertaking requires peculiar skill, what is the mandatary's undertaking and what his responsibility?
19. What is a commodatum?
20. Does it apply to articles consumed in the use?
21. How of stocks loaned by brokers and not to be specifically returned?
22. What becomes of the increment of the thing loaned, as the young of animals?
23. What is a pledge?
24. What the distinction between mortgage, pledge, and lien?
25. What is essential to a pledge?
26. How can delivery sufficient be made of goods at sea?
27. What suits can pledgee bring?
28. Can pledgee hold for other debts than that for which it was given?
29. Can he use the pledge?
30. What care must he take; *e.g.*, if a promissory note be pledged, what must he do as to demand, etc.?
31. What if pledgee sell stocks?
32. What is the pledgee's remedy if the debt is not paid?
33. How can pledgee acquire absolute property?
34. How can pledgee of paper transfer it?
35. How is the pledge terminated?

36. If pledgee has sold unlawfully what is the pledgor's remedy?
37. How is the pledge discharged?

- –

PARSONS ON CONTRACTS.

Chapter II, Secs. 5, 6, 7.

1. What is a *locatio?*
2. What degree of care is required? Examples.
3. *Locatio rei* is what?
4. What is essential to it?
5. Can bailor interfere with the use during the term agreed for the hire?
6. How if the bailment be abused?
7. If a thing is hired for a particular object, what is the owner's duty as to fitness?
8. For what subsequent expense is he answerable, and for what the hirer?
9. How of property in care of bailor's servant, as if I hire a coach and he sends a driver?
10. How if the bailment is diverted from the use for which hired?
11. How if damage results from deviation from the use designed?
12. What interest has the bailee?
13. Can he sell or mortgage as agent for the real owner?
14. How of hired chattels fastened permanently to the freehold?
15. If furniture is hired with a house, by what law is it governed?
16. If a chattel is delivered to be worked on, what is the implied obligation of the bailee?
17. If the materials are destroyed before the work is done, when is the workman entitled to pay and when not?
18. How, if he agrees to make me a table out of lumber furnished by me and it is burnt before being finished?
19. If I furnish cloth for a coat and the tailor the thread and buttons, on whom does the loss fall?
20. How if the case be reversed?

21. If I furnish grain and the miller is to return so many bushels of flour, is this a bailment, and on whom does the loss fall in case of its destruction?
22. How if the bailee confuse his goods with the bailor's?
23. If a workman is hired generally to work on an article, as a machine, and his work is useless, can he recover?
24. If it is badly done, but accepted?
25. If he is prevented by the employer or by accident from completing, how?
26. If employed by the day, even if he refuses to go on?
27. If employed by the job and he refuses, can he recover anything?
28. If employed by special contract to do certain work and for a certain price, if the contract is not performed strictly, what remedy has he?
29. If the contract is deviated from by consent or partially executed, how?
30. If the work is left unfinished or deviates from the contract through the workman's fault, can he recover on a *quantum meruit?*
31. If the work is done properly, and only the price remains to be paid, must the suit be on special contract?
32. When more costly materials are used than required, can they be recovered for?
33. If departures are with consent of parties, what is the rule as to price?
34. If one act as carrier and warehouseman, when does one character end and the other begin?
35. When goods arrive at the end of the route and are held for delivery, what is he, and what his responsibility?
36. When goods are received to be forwarded, how?
37. If goods in a bailee's hands are claimed by a stranger, what must he do?
38. What is the obligation of an innkeeper?
39. What is an inn for this purpose?
40. What will exempt an innkeeper from responsibility for his guest's goods?

41. How soon does the liability begin?
42. Who are travellers in the sense of the law?
43. How of boarders?
44. If one sends his goods alone, how? Or leaves them?
45. What lien has the innkeeper?
46. How of a horse sent to livery?
47. If the livery man is also an innkeeper?
48. How of another's goods held by the guest?
49. What is a carrier?
50. What is a common carrier?
51. What is his responsibility, and what its origin?
52. What is the act of God?
53. How as to inherent faults in the articles carried?
54. How if carrier's negligence contributes to the accident?
55. What are the public enemies meant by this rule?
56. What is the responsibility of carriers of passengers?
57. When is a ship a common carrier?
58. When the railroad is in the hands of a receiver is the company liable as a common carrier?
59. What are a carrier's duties as to receipt of freights and rights as to his pay?
60. What discriminations can he make?
61. Sum up his liabilities?
62. If goods are shipped C. O. D. is the carrier bound to collect?

PARSONS ON CONTRACTS.

Book III, Chapter 11, Secs. 7 to 16, inclusive, and end.

1. When does the carrier's liability begin?
2. Where must the delivery be made to bind the carrier?
3. What notice must be given?
4. How if goods be delivered to a carrier to be kept till further order?
5. If a ship be chartered to carry for the public, who is the carrier, the owner or charterer?

6. When does the carrier's liability end?
7. That of a railroad company?
8. What is the liability when goods are kept in the depot?
9. How if goods be delivered to the wrong person?
10. Does the carrier insure delivery at a certain time?
11. How if he contracts expressly?
12. If a carrier receive goods directed beyond his route, does this bind him to deliver beyond?
13. What is the carrier's liability if the passenger keeps charge of his property?
14. For what property of a passenger is a carrier bound?
15. How does the owner's improper interference with the delivery of the goods affect the carrier's responsibility?
16. How if they are thrown overboard to save the ship?
17. How if the carrier pay for the goods lost, is he entitled to his freight?
18. If one without title to goods ships them on the railroad, is the carrier entitled to his freight as against the owner?
19. How if they are carried where the owner wishes them carried?
20. What if consignee refuses to receive?
21. Where several carriers unite their routes and share profits, what is their liability?
22. How in case of through lines without division of losses and expenses?
23. In case of connecting lines, who can be sued by shipper in case of loss in England, and how in this country?
24. If one company allows another's trains to run over its roads, is it liable for losses on the trains?
25. What is the carrier's obligation to a passenger?
26. Does a free pass make any difference in the liability of the carrier?
27. How if expressed to be on condition of non-liability for neglect of agents?
28. Where is the burden of proof, in case of injury to a passenger?
29. How as to a stranger and intruder?

30. What is the effect of the passenger's own neglect contributing to his injury?
31. Must infants and adults exercise the same care?
32. What is the general rule as to degree of care on the part of a railroad company?
33. What its responsibility for torts committed by its agents and officers?
34. What must a passenger do?
35. If he is expelled for not paying fare, must he be admitted again if he tenders it?
36. What must the company do as to disorderly or offensive persons?
37. Is a railroad company liable for injuries to property from sparks, etc.?
38. What if a passenger leave a car while in motion and is injured, can he recover?
39. What is the carrier's liability as to the passenger's baggage?
40. How if a trunk is sent on and not carried with the passenger?
41. Can a carrier modify his common law liability by special agreement?
42. In what particular cases?
43. How of a mere notice that he will not be liable, etc.?
44. How as to liability beyond the carrier's route?
45. Can the carrier confine his business to any particular kind of freight?
46. How far is a carrier bound by his advertised times of departing and arriving?
47. Can he by contract exempt himself from the consequences of his own negligence?
48. Can he discriminate between ticket and car-fares?
49. How if the office be closed and the passenger is unable to procure a ticket?
50. Is carrier responsible to a servant for injuries from neglect of another servant?
51. What is the limit to the rule to which courts incline?
52. Are city railway companies common carriers?

PARSONS ON CONTRACTS.

Book III, Chapter 12.

1. How far is a telegraph company a common carrier?
2. Is it an insurer?
3. What is its duty as to equipment, accuracy and promptness, priority, secrecy?
4. Are these messages confidential communications?
5. What is its duty as to delivery?
6. With whom is its contract?
7. May they limit their liability for negligence?
8. If the sender is agent of the receiver is the contract held to be with the latter?
9. What action can the receiver maintain?
10. Are contracts completed by telegraph of acceptance as in case of letters?
11. Is one bound to give notice by telegraph?
12. Do telegrams make up a memorandum under the Statute of Frauds?
13. What is the measure of damages in case of mistake, as when goods meanwhile rise in price?

PARSONS ON CONTRACTS.

Book III, Chapter 13, Secs. 1 to 6 inclusive.

1. What is a patent?
2. How does it differ from a monopoly?
3. To whom may patents be issued under the act of 1870?
4. What originality of invention is necessary on the part of the applicant?
5. How if the applicant has adopted suggestions, as to details, from others?
6. What if the invention has been patented abroad?

7. What if the inventor has abandoned the invention, and what amounts to an abandonment?
8. What is a caveat and its effect?
9. What is the first requisite of an invention to entitle its author to a patent?
10. What of the application of old inventions to new uses? Examples.
11. What if the patent embraces something that is not original and something that is?
12. What are reissues, and under what circumstances are they allowed?
13. What is a disclaimer?
14. What is the next requirement besides novelty?
15. Is it necessary that it shall have required thought and invention?
16. What amount of novelty will suffice if a useful result is produced? Examples. Substitution of one kind of coal for another?
17. Suppose no change of result has followed?
18. How of change of form of machinery?
19. How of new combinations of existing machinery?
20. How of improvements in mere ornaments which will make them sell better?
21. Is a product patentable as well as the machine producing it?
22. What signification is given to the term *manufacture* in England?
23. What is meant by a *process?*
24. What was Watt's invention for saving fuel by preventing the escape of heat from boilers?
25. What Neilson's improvement by using hot air in a blast-furnace?
26. Is a process patentable, *eo nomine*, in this country?
27. Under what terms within the act of Congress is it embraced?
28. Is an abstract principle—a law of physics—a function of matter patentable?
29. How does it become patentable?

30. How do ours and the English courts differ in their views on this subject?
31. What was held about Prof. Morse's discovery?
32. Can known machinery be used in the application of a newly discovered law, and a patent be had for the process?
33. What is the difference between a machine and a process?
34. The arts of tanning, dyeing, applying caoutchouc, etc., are what?
35. If various machines are used for producing a result, what is the subject of a patent?
36. What is meant by a double use?
37. Will a new process producing better results, which consists merely in omitting materials used before, be patentable?
38. What is embraced by the terms new and useful art?
39. What is a machine?
40. Does machine include a combination of old machines?
41. Is a mere improvement in an existing machine patentable?
42. What right has the patentee of the improvement?
43. What does the term manufacture embrace?
44. When is a tool a manufacture, and when a machine?
45. What is a composition?
46. What is the rule as to unity of invention in a patent?
47. How if a combination and also the several machines making it are embraced within the same patent?
48. How if several improvements in a machine are embraced within the same patent?
49. How about patents to several persons?
50. Can an inventor join another in one patent with himself?
51. What is the first step to be taken by an applicant?
52. What must he state in his petition?
53. What is the specification, and what relation has it to the letters-patent?
54. What if there is a plain repugnance between the patent and the specification?
55. What are questions for the court and what for the jury in a patent cause?
56. What are the objects of the specification?

57. What is the object of letting the public know what is claimed?
58. What if it embraces something old?
59. What particularity is needed as to substance used, etc.?
60. What is the effect of unnecessary details and ingredients being stated?
61. How if he really uses cheaper materials than those described?
62. How if the claim be for a mere principle?
63. If the process or machine is described, how far will the patent include variations?
64. What amount of clearness is necessary in so describing the invention as to enable others to use it?
65. Is it sufficient to make it comprehensible to the most scientific only?
66. Must it be so to all the world or only those versed in the art?
67. How if it cannot be used without having to exercise further invention?
68. How if any, however slight, omission is made?
69. What remedy is there for accidental vagueness, excess, or deficiency of description?
70. How is the right to recover in a suit for infringement affected by the excess in specification?

PARSONS ON CONTRACTS.

Chapter XIII, Sec. 7 to the end.

1. What assignment of patents may be made?
2. Can the invention be sold before the patent?
3. Who must make application in such case?
4. Can the assignment be conditional?
5. What assignments have to be recorded?
6. What of licenses?
7. What rights has an assignee of a fractional interest?
8. What the grantee of a fractional interest?
9. Does a license give any exclusive right?

10. Can a licensee, to use a machine, practice the invention beyond the use of the machine?
11. What is the test whether an instrument is an assignment or license?
12. What becomes of the patent in case of bankruptcy?
13. Does an assignment imply a warrant of the validity of the patent?
14. Does the assignee become a partner of the assignor by assignment?
15. What are the rights of the assignee of a fractional interest?
16. How if he undersells the assignor?
17. What are assignee's rights in case of renewal upon surrender and reissue?
18. How as to extension after the expiration of the original term?
19. How if assignee is in the use of a patented machine when the patent expires?
20. Can he keep it in repair?
21. Can assignee again assign?
22. Can licensee assign?
23. Can he divide or apportion his license among several?
24. If a sum of money be payable for a license, can payment be refused because of the invalidity of the patent?
25. How if payments have been made?
26. How of periodical payments of which some have been made?
27. Where there is a sectional grant, what can be done with manufactured articles?
28. What are the rights of a purchaser of a patented machine or article? Can he repair it?
29. How of the right to manufacture a patented machine?
30. Is the purchaser of products of a patented machine from a known infringer an infringer himself?
31. Who is to be sued in such case?
32. Can the grantee sue in his own name?
33. Who sues for the exclusive licensee?
34. Who must sue for infringement, where fractional interests are assigned?

35. Can one assign, with right to assignee to sue in his own name, the right to use the patent for certain kinds of manufacture?
36. At what time must a person be interested to have a right of action under the law?
37. What must be averred in the declaration in an action for infringement?
38. What is an interference, and in what cases does it arise?
39. What remedy by suit is provided for such cases?
40. What rights does the patent give to the inventor?
41. What amounts to an infringement?
42. What is necessary to make a case of infringement?
43. If the patent is for a combination of machines, will the omission of any one be an infringement in the use of the others?
44. Could the plaintiff show that to be useless?
45. If the patent is for a machine, to what does the patent extend?
46. Is making for experiment only, or amusement, an infringement?
47. Is the mechanic who makes a part of a machine, or the merchant who sells the materials, the infringer?
48. If the sheriff sells a machine as the property of patentee or assignee, does the right to use it pass to the buyer?
49. Is the officer or buyer guilty of infringement?
50. Is hiring a machine to another to be used by him an infringement?
51. Is buying goods in good faith from one wrongfully using a patented machine?
52. Is selling the product of a patented machine an infringement if the seller has no interest in the machine?
53. What does a patent for a composition of matter cover?
54. Is one who buys and consumes a patented *product* an infringer?
55. What is meant by mechanical equivalents?
56. Suppose the mechanical equivalent, however, makes an improvement?

57. If the patent is for a manufacture, is it an infringement to make it by a new process?
58. What is understood by the principle of an invention?
59. How does this differ from a principle in nature?
60. If the proportions of materials are described as necessary in the specification, is it any infringement to use them in different proportions?
61. If there is a single patent for several improvements, is the use of any one of them an infringement?
62. Is a suit for infringement defeated by showing the mere inutility of part of the invention?
63. Is an invention infringed upon by its use before the patent issues?
64. How of such use after surrender and renewal?
65. Is notice of renewal in such case necessary?
66. What defences are allowed by statute?
67. What others can be made?
68. On whom is the burden as to the defence of deception, etc.?
69. What kind of previous printed publication describing the invention will suffice to defeat recovery?
70. What is proof of abandonment to the public?
71. What kind of communication to others will or will not be?
72. What is the remedy in equity against infringers?
73. On what grounds does equity interfere?
74. What must the bill allege in addition to what a declaration at law must?
75. Will injunction issue before actual infringement?
76. Is notice required?
77. What is the usual proceeding when the patent is new or the right doubtful?
78. What other practice prevails besides enjoining, where that would irreparably injure the party?
79. What is the final relief?
80. Why must plaintiff ask the interlocutory injunctions?
81. What of profits?
82. Will defendant be chargeable with profits he might have made with due diligence?

83. In case of assignment of the whole interest for royalty, and default of payment, what is the remedy?
84. How in case of license and periodical payments?
85. Will the use of an article patented in this country, but lawfully acquired abroad, be enjoined?
86. What would be the measure of damages in an infringement suit?
87. What may the court do?
88. What is the remedy in interference cases?

PARSONS ON CONTRACTS.

Book III, Chapters 14 and 15.

1. Who is entitled to take a copyright?
2. For what term of years?
3. What formality is required?
4. Do any letters patent issue?
5. How do they differ from patents as to renewal?
6. What will defeat a copyright?
7. Is the delivery of a lecture such a publication as will?
8. How of the printing alone of books?
9. How of the representation of a play?
10. What could the hearers do without infringement?
11. What does a copyright cover—the author's ideas or their expression?
12. Are newspapers, labels, price-currents covered by the term *book?*
13. What amount of invention or novelty is required?
14. Is a selection and arrangement of the materials sufficient?
15. In whom resides the right to copyright letters?
16. How of works immoral or irreligious?
17. What of law reports?
18. What right of assignment has the author?
19. How before or after copyrighting?

20. What is the effect of an assignment?
21. What if one gratuitously furnishes comments and notes to the owner of a copyrighted book, can he afterwards copyright them?
22. If one is employed by a manager to write a play for his theatre, may the author copyright it?
23. Does a general assignment carry this right to the extension also?
24. What is an infringement of a copyright?
25. What is the penalty of infringement?
26. What is necessary to make an infringement?
27. How of reviews and criticisms?
28. How if the pirated material is only part of a new work?
29. Will the publication of the whole be enjoined?
30. Is a translation of a book into a foreign language an infringement?
31. How if translated back again?
32. How of compilations?
33. What would be an infringement in such case?
34. What of abridgments?
35. What abridgment would be an infringement?
36. In what cases would equity decline to interfere by injunction?
37. How if a work has only a temporary value?
38. What exclusive right to trade-marks is given by the law?
39. What is the object of the trade-mark?
40. What are the subjects of trade-marks?
41. What is essential to a proper trade-mark?
42. How of terms merely describing the articles?
43. Can the producer appropriate a word in common use as his exclusive property?
44. How of a new word?
45. What may be used as a trade-mark?
46. Can a seller use a trade-mark as distinct from a manufacturer?
47. How of the unauthorized use of a party's name on another hotel or conveyance than his own?

48. Will one who has used deception in connection with his trade-mark be protected?
49. Can a trade-mark be bequeathed or assigned?
50. Can it be used apart from its original application?
51. How in case of a sale of a business and good-will?
52. What amounts to an infringement of a trade-mark?
53. Is corrupt intention necessary?
54. What is the remedy?

PARSONS ON CONTRACTS.

SHIPPING.

Book III, Chapter 16.

1. Under a building contract, when does title to a ship pass?
2. How if partial payments are made during the work?
3. What rights are acquired by payment of instalments?
4. What lien has the builder?
5. What lien has a material-man by the maritime law?
6. How of American and English law, when repairs are made in the home port?
7. How when they are made in a foreign port?
8. How if the owner has an agent in the foreign port ready to pay?
9. How is this lien enforced, and is possession necessary to it?
10. Is one State foreign to another for this purpose?
11. What modification of the lien is made as to domestic vessels by the Supreme Court rules?
12. What kind of claim is entitled to this lien?
13. What is the evidence of title to a ship?
14. Is writing necessary?
15. What is required by act of Congress of 1850?
16. For what object is written evidence of title necessary?
17 What is the relation of part owners to each other
18 What control has a part owner over the property?

19. What of a majority?
20. How will a court of admiralty interfere as to the management?
21. What is a ship's husband, and who may be?
22. What are his duties?
23. What authority has he to make contracts to bind the owners?
24. Has a part owner any lien for advances?
25. Is there any warranty of title or fitness on a sale of a ship?
26. What is the effect of retaining possession on the vendor's part after sale?
27. What kind of delivery can be made where the ship is at sea?
28. What would defeat attaching creditors of vendor?
29. When has the master authority to sell?
30. What constitutes the justifying necessity?
31. What is the effect of a decree of sale in admiralty?
32. What exception to the rule?
33. What is the effect of a mortgagee's taking possession?
34. What is a bottomry bond given for?
35. How does it differ from a mortgage or pledge?
36. How from other contracts of loan?
37. What if the money is returnable in any event?
38. How is the bottomry contract enforced?
39. Can the bottomry contract be secured by other collateral contracts or mortgages on other property?
40. How are these contracts made the means of securing usurious interest?
41. If several successive bottomry bonds are given, which has the priority?
42. When can the master and when the owner give a bottomry bond?
43. What inquiry must lender make before advancing on bottomry?
44. Can a master give a bottomry bond for an antecedent indebtedness?
45. Does the bond give a personal claim against the owner?
46. What will discharge the bond?
47. How if the ship is lost through the master's fault?

48. What is the respondentia bond?
49. What is freight, and what is the contract to carry called?
50. What engagements are implied on the owner's part by the receipt of goods on board?
51. What rights does he acquire?
52. Can the owner withdraw the goods after they are shipped?
53. When is freight considered earned?
54. What exceptions?
55. Where the goods arrive in a damaged condition, under what circumstances is freight due?
56. How if the entire contents of barrels, etc., are lost from the perils of the sea?
57. When is part of the freight payable?
58. When is it apportioned where part of the cargo arrives?
59. What are the reciprocal remedies of owner and shipper?
60. When does the lien for freight commence?
61. What is a bill of lading?
62. Who may be the consignee?
63. Can the master bind the owner by a bill of lading given without any shipment of the goods?
64. How if the bill is assigned to a third person for value and without notice?
65. Who has the right of action on a bill of lading, consignor or consignee?
66. How far is the bill of lading negotiable?
67. When is consignee entitled to the goods?
68. Is the lien for freight lost by delivery of the goods?
69. What may consignee do if only part of the cargo arrives, where the freight is a gross charge for the whole?
70. If he receives a part, has he any action for non-delivery of the rest?
71. What must the ship-owner show to exempt himself from responsibility for the goods?
72. If he pays the value of goods lost, is he entitled to freight?
73. If the voyage is interrupted by superior authority, as an embargo, is freight earned?

74. If the voyage is ended but delivery is prevented, how?
75. If a ship is detained at an intermediate port, what may the owner do as to forwarding the goods?
76. Who is liable for any extra freight that may be necessary?
77. What if the ship-owner refuses to tranship when he can?
78. If the goods are tendered to the shipper at an intermediate port, what may he do?
79. Can the master sell when the ship is arrested at an intermediate port?
80. What is a charter-party?
81. If in the master's name, does it bind the owners personally?
82. With whom does the legal possession remain when a charter-party is executed?
83. What are the usual stipulations?
84. What is the security to each for performance?
85. What is demurrage?
86. What remedy for failure to provide the cargo within the time agreed?
87. Is delay from superior force a ground for demurrage?
88. What will discharge the charter-party?
89. What is the effect of a temporary blockade?
90. What liability does the bill of lading impose?
91. In what respect does it resemble the common law liability of the common carrier?
92. For what losses is the ship-owner or charterer responsible to the shipper?
93. Is fire one of the extraordinary perils?
94. How if caused by lightning?
95. In cases of collision, without the fault of either party, where does the loss fall?
96. How where both parties are to blame?
97. How if there is blame, but it is uncertain where it belongs?
98. How if the loss results from the fault of the suffering party?
99. How if from the fault of the other?

100. What was the common law rule where the fault was mutual?
101. Where the loss is divided, in case of mutual fault, how is it apportioned?
102. What is the presumption in case of collision between a steamer and a sailer?
103. What is the remedy in admiralty in case of collision?
104. What remedy has the shipper of goods where they are injured or lost through collision by the ship-owner's fault?
105. How if they are lost in collision from the fault of the other vessel?
106. Has the shipper a remedy against the vessel in default?
107. What is salvage?
108. What security and remedy has the salvor?
109. In what case may a salvor interfere?
110. What are the cases proper for marine salvage?
111. What is derelict?
112. Does the case arise when master and crew voluntarily give up the ship to the salvor?
113. What persons are entitled to claim salvage?
114. Can passengers?
115. When may one of the crew?
116. A pilot?
117. If part of a ship's crew engage in the actual work of saving, are the rest entitled to salvage?
118. How as to the owner of the relieving ship?
119. What are double sets of salvors?
120. Do the first salvors, in such case, lose their reward?
121. Who are entitled to share in salvage?
122. Is there constructive assistance?
123. Is salvage allowed for saving life?
124. What amount is allowed for salvage?
125. What property pays the salvage?
126. Does the freight?
127. When are salvors precluded from claiming?
128. What is meant by general average?
129. What property is to contribute to it?
130. Is a loss caused by the elements a subject of general average?

131. What is essential to make a case for general average?
132. If a jettison is made by the master, but the cargo could not have been saved anyhow, is this a case for average?
133. Is a loss by surrender of goods to pirates, as a ransom, a case for average?
134. Where injury to a vessel is caused in saving cargo, is it a case for salvage?
135. How of wages and premiums in seeking a port of repair?
136. Is there a difference where the injury was caused by tempest or voluntary sacrifice?
137. Where the loss is from a decree of salvage, is it a subject of average?
138. By what standard of value is the loss averaged?
139. Does freight contribute?
140. Is the loss of freight or goods thrown overboard itself a subject of average?
141. Where is the average to be adjusted?
142. What authority has the master in a foreign port as to chartering the ship, etc.?
143. Is the master himself responsible on his contracts?
144. What remedy is there on a charter-party in his own name?
145. How far are owners responsible for the master's negligent torts?
146. How far is the master responsible for goods shipped?
147. How far is he bound to the mariners?
148. What right has the master in regard to securing his advances or securing himself against liabilities for advances?
149. Can a master delegate his authority?
150. What power has he over the cargo when he can neither carry nor send it forward?
151. If all the cargo be sold, can any part of the loss be charged to the cargo?
152. How are shipping articles generally interpreted?
153. What lien have seamen, and how does it rank as to others?
154. What relation have wages to freight?

155. If a ship is bound out and home, and performs the outward voyage, but is lost on the way home, are there any wages earned?
156. How if parts of the cargo are delivered at different ports?
157. How if the freight is paid in advance?
158. How if the voyage is lost through the misconduct of master or owner?
159. What is the relation of the pilot to the ship?
160. What of losses from neglect to employ pilots?

PARSONS ON CONTRACTS.

Book III, Chapter 17.

1. What is the contract of maritime insurance?
2. What called?
3. What form is necessary?
4. What is the consideration?
5. How does it become also a contract of the insured?
6. Is he bound to expose to the risk insured against after receiving the policy?
7. If not, is any premium payable?
8. What are the stipulations on the part of the insured?
9. If agent insure without authority, can principal ratify after loss?
10. How does insured forfeit the policy?
12. Can a policy be assigned?
12. What is the subject-matter of the insurance?
13. What is the effect of transfer of property after insurance?
14. How if insured be a trustee?
15. How does assignment of policy operate if consent of the insurer is required and not given?
16. How of an assignment for the benefit of creditors?
17. How of assignment after loss has occurred?
18. How of an assignment by one to other joint owners?
19. If a ship sails but immediately returns, is the premium due?

20. If the premium is paid but the voyage abandoned, can the premium be recovered?
21. What are open and what valued policies?
22. In the latter, if part of goods are not shipped, is part of premium to be returned?
23. What interest must be named in the policy?
24. What can be insured?
25. How must the thing be described?
26. Can a policy be made to cover loss already incurred?
27. "Lost or not lost" means what?
28. When does the risk terminate?
29. What does an open policy cover?
30. What is double insurance? Over insurance?
31. How did the various underwriters pay in case of loss?
32. In case the second policy is expressed to cover what is not already covered by the prior policy, what is the meaning?
33. In case, then, the property diminishes in value, what is the effect?
34. What is the object of requiring other insurances to be notified to the insurers?
35. Is it double insurances for mortgagor and mortgagee to insure their respective interests?
36. What is reinsurance, and its object?
37. Is there any privity between insured and the reinsured?
38. What must be proven against the latter?
39. Where a vessel is insured, is the underwriter responsible for losses from neglect of crew?
40. How if this neglect caused loss by the perils of the sea?
41. What are ordinary and extraordinary risks, and are the former covered by the insurance?
42. Does it cover destruction by fire to save from the enemy?
43. When is general average a loss within the policy?
44. What is a total loss?
45. What is abandonment?
46. Can the underwriter pursue the voyage and earn the profit if he can save the vessel?
47. In case of partial loss, what is the duty of the underwriter?

48. If an injured vessel is repaired with new materials what does the insurer pay for them?
49. What is a warranty in a policy?
50. If the fact be false, does materiality make any difference?
51. What is the effect of breach?
52. What are representations?
53. What the effect of a false one?
54. What if innocent?
55. What are implied warranties on the part of the insured?
56. What is deviation, and its effect?
57. What of deviation from necessity?
58. In what case can there be no deviation?

PARSONS ON CONTRACTS.

Book III, Chapters 18 and 19.

1. In fire insurance, what is the security of the insured?
2. What is the arrangement in mutual companies?
3. Does the distinction between warranties and representations apply?
4. How far is the description of the property in a policy a warranty for the future?
5. How do alterations in a house affect the policy?
6. How if destroyed from increased risk during the alteration?
7. What warranties would be regarded as continuing, and what not?
8. What is necessary to make a misrepresentation avoid a policy?
9. What if it is stipulated that false answers on particular matters shall avoid?
10. What interest is sufficient?
11. Is a mere expectancy?
12. How as to a mortgagor?
13. How if the buildings are burned but the land is sufficient security?
14. If insurer pays mortgagee, is he entitled to subrogation?

15. May mortgagee still sue for the debt?
16. What is the usual form of the contract?
17. What is the practice of factors as to description of the goods?
18. Is a lien an insurable interest?
19. What if the property is already destroyed, or in imminent danger of it?
20. Can they make it retrospective?
21. How if exposed to a dangerous fire at the time?
22. What loss is covered by insurance against fire?
23. Is one from steam or explosion from another house blown up?
24. How as to a gunpowder explosion caused by fire?
25. How as to injuries from water, or in removing goods?
26. How of theft?
27. How of blowing up to prevent the spread of the fire?
28. If underwriters elect to rebuild, what is their liability?
29. How are damages limited in case of failure?
30. Is negligence of the insured or servants a defence to the underwriters?
31. What is the effect of alienation, total or partial?
32. Has a mortgage any such effect?
33. Assignment by voluntary bankruptcy?
34. What standard of value determines the claim of the assured?
35. In case of partial destruction, if the repairs cost less than the sum insured, what of the balance?
36. In case of double insurance, what do the insurers pay?
37. Does the notice required apply to subsequent as well as prior insurance?
38. How if this be void?
39. What is the effect of not giving the notice required?
40. If the mortgagee insures himself, and the mortgagor also, for his benefit, is this double insurance?
41. Reinsurance is what?
42. Will conditions in policies as to time of demand and suit be binding?
43. What difference is there between maritime and fire insurance in case of partial loss?

44. Where one insures his life, to whom is the money payable on his death?
45. Where he insures another's life, how on the death of the insured?
46. What effect is given to the answers of an applicant for insurance to the printed forms of questions?
47. The general statement that he is in good health covers what?
48. Is the company bound by the certificate of its own physician?
49. If one insures another, is he bound by his answers?
50. What effect have exceptions of certain pursuits, etc., in the policy?
51. Is interest in another's life necessary to entitle one to insure?
52. What is sufficient interest, where required?
53. Where the creditor collects an insurance, can the debtor's representatives refuse to pay the debt?
54. Is the insurer paying subrogated to the creditor?
55. Can creditors interfere with an insurance for wife's benefit?
56. When does the risk begin?
57. How in case of bargain to insure?
58. If a renewal premium is not paid, but the agent promises to make another policy, or charges himself with the premium, is the company bound?
59. How if so many days are allowed after expiration of policy, and the insured dies in the interval?

PARSONS ON CONTRACTS.

PART II, CHAPTER I.

1. In what cases does the court and in what does the jury determine the meaning of a contract?
2. What is the cardinal ethical rule of interpretation?
3. How far is this modified by common law?
4. How if a contract cannot operate in one way, but can in another

5. Take the case of bargain and sale for love and affection?
6. Against whom is the contract most strongly construed?
7. What is the rule as to inconsistent clauses in deeds, wills, and other instruments?
8. What is the effect of express contract of title in a lease on the legal implications from the word demise?
9. How if a mortgage expressly conveys *some* of the fixtures?
10. If printed forms are filled up, to which is most weight given, the printing or writing?
11. In what cases is a contract severable?
12. What is the right of rescission in case of entire contracts?
13. In case of part performance, what is a remedy if a party is prevented from completing?
14. How when deviations are made by consent?
15. Suppose a party performs partly, and then refuses to complete, but the fruit of the part performance is retained by the other party, can the first recover for the work done?
16. When were mutual covenants considered independent, and when dependent?
17. Is parol evidence admissible to change the terms of a contract?
18. How as to fraud in reducing to writing?
19. What is the rule as to *falsa demonstratio?*
20. Is parol evidence admissible to show the contract other than the law implies?
21. What as to contemporaneous writings?
22. Can it be shown by parol that recitals are incorrect?
23. That the consideration is different?
24. How as to alterations?
25. How as to instruments under seal?
26. How as to waiver of conditions, etc.?
27. Additional consideration?
28. Receipts?
29. How is this rule as to third persons?
30. What is the rule as to patent and latent ambiguity?

PARSONS ON CONTRACTS.

Part II, Chapter 2.

1. What force and effect has the law of one State in another?
2. By what law is the capacity of a contracting party determined?
3. How as to the validity and interpretation of the contract?
4. What is the comity of nations?
5. Would a contract here to pay interest, at 10 per centum per annum, be enforced in a State where the interest is lower?
6. Would a contract here to pay 20 per centum, which is unlawful here, be enforced in California, if lawful there?
7. What law governs the descent and transfer of real estate?
8. If one contract a debt, valid there, in another State, secured by deed of trust here, and the interest would be usurious here, what is the consequence?
9. What law governs as to personal capacity, *i.e.*, slavery, marriage, infancy, apprenticeship, etc.?
10. If a party under age by the law of his domicil, contract elsewhere, where he is of full age, for that purpose, which law governs?
11. What is one's domicil?
12. What the wife's? Child's?
13. How is it changed?
14. Can one have two domicils?
15. What determines the question, when he resides in different places at different times of the year?
16. If the contract is made in one place, but is to be performed in another, the laws of which place govern?
17. How of a promissory note in New York, payable in Washington?
18. When a note is dated at one place, though made at another, to which does it belong?
19. If a New York merchant gives notes in Boston for goods, to which city does the contract belong?

20. If a note be given in New York payable in Boston, how?
21. If a note be given generally, not dated, at New York, how?
22. How if dated at New York or payable there?
23. What law determines the sufficiency of discharges?
24. Does the law of the place apply to torts?
25. What is the *lex fori?*
26. A deed with a scroll being a specialty here, but a simple contract in New York, what action may be brought on it in New York?
27. Is the defence of limitations governed by the law of the place of the contract, or law of the forum?
28. What if lapse of time by the law of the place of contract extinguishes the debt?
29. How, when by the *lex loci contractus,* one acquires complete title to personal chattels, by possession?
30. Does the Statute of Frauds belong to the *lex loci* or *lex fori?*
31. How of set-off?
32. By what law is the validity of marriage governed?
33. How if deemed incestuous by the law of another State?
34. How if parties go abroad and marry to evade local law?
35. By what law are the incidents of marriage governed?
36. By what law, the question of legitimacy in case of realty and personalty?
37. What determines the wife's title in husband's property?
38. By what law is the validity of divorce governed?
39. What jurisdiction is necessary to make a divorce valid; must both parties be within the State?
40. What is the nature of a decree of divorce, is it *in personam* or *in rem?*
41. How if one go abroad to get a divorce, in fraud of the law of his domicil?
42. What effect had a foreign judgment at common law?
43. What difference between suing on it and offering it in defence?
44. What of an interlocutory judgment?
45. What merger is there of the original cause of action?

46. Can a foreign *lis pendens* be pleaded in abatement even?
47. What is the effect of a judgment of another State in this country?

PARSONS ON CONTRACTS.

Part II, Chapter 3.

1. Is an attorney at law, employed to collect, authorized to receive payment?
2. Is an auctioneer?
3. A wife?
4. Can payment be made to principal, if the agent is known to have claims on the fund?
5. Can a debtor set off a demand on the agent, known to be such, against the principal?
6. Can payment be made to one of joint creditors not partners?
7. How of partners?
8. How of executors and trustees?
9. How of joint depositors in bank?
10. If partial payment be made to one, can the debtor pay the balance to the other?
11. Is part payment of a debt, receipted in full, a bar?
12. If so, under what circumstances?
13. How of compromises of doubtful claims?
14. What is a debtor's duty as to payment?
15. Would mailing the money be payment?
16. Will payment in bank bills be sufficient?
17. How of payment in forged bills?.
18. How if the bank be insolvent but has not actually failed, without the knowledge of either?
19. How if the bank has actually failed?
20. How if notes are taken in payment for goods at the time of sale, instead of in payment of an existing debt?
21. How is payment by check considered?

22. How if a bank fails before the check is presented?
23. What of payment by note?
24. What if the note is indorsed over?
25. When, if at all, can the creditor sue on the original consideration, in such a case?
26. How of a third person's note?
27. What is the duty of holder as to demand, etc., and what the consequence of neglect?
28. What is payment by delegation?
29. How about deposits with stakeholders, and what payments will discharge them?
30. How of deposits with auctioneer, on sale?
31. What if stakeholder pay over to one party in advance of decision, on receiving indemnity?
32. How is money paid, to be applied, when there are several distinct debts?
33. How if collected by execution?
34. If the debtor fails to make application, how?
35. If neither party makes the application, how will it be done?
36. How will the law apply when one of several debts is disputed?
37. What limitations are there on the creditor's right of application?
38. How as to debts held in different rights? how where one is not due?
39. How as to items not suable?
40. How when one debt is barred by limitations?
41. How when payment is made by a third person and not the debtor?
42. How will the court apply, as between good and precarious securities?
43. How between mortgage debt and one unsecured?
44. How between one bearing interest and one not?
45. How where one debt binds a surety?
46. How is interest to be computed?
47. What is the difference between the two modes?
48. When must a tender be shown?
49. In what kind of case could tender be proven?

50. Can tender be pleaded with general issue?
51. What is the effect of tender?
52. What amount should be tendered?
53. What if more than the debt be tendered?
54. In what must it be made?
55. When is it good in bank notes?
56. Must the money be produced?
57. When is production excused?
58. Is a conditional tender good?
59. How if on condition of giving a release?
60. What is the effect of a subsequent demand and refusal?
61. When specific articles are to be tendered, what is the debtor's duty?
62. If goods are at the time and place agreed, and the buyer is not there, what?
63. What was the effect of a tender of goods?
64. If the debtor had the option to pay in goods or money and failed to deliver the goods, what is the effect?

PARSONS ON CONTRACTS.

Part II, Chapter 3, continued.

1. What is a release?
2. Must it be under seal, and why?
3. Suppose not, but it is for a consideration, what would it be?
4. What of a general covenant not to sue?
5. What of a covenant not to sue for a limited time?
6. What of covenant, generally, not to sue one of several?
7. On what can a release operate?
8. How of future causes of action?
9. How of contract rights depending on future conditions?
10. Can a general release under seal be qualified by parol evidence?

11. Can a release by another, beneficially interested, be pleaded against a plaintiff having the legal right of action?
12. When is a release by operation of law?
13. How of the taking of higher security as collateral?
14. What of alteration by a stranger?
15. By holder?
16. How does adding a seal affect the contract?
17. What is the presumption in case of alteration?
18. How would title under a deed be affected by an alteration in it?
19. How as to the covenants?
20. What is the effect of pendency of another suit for the same cause of action?
21. How of a suit abroad?
22. How of attachment of the debt by garnishment abroad?
23. What is the defence of a former judgment?
24. What is necessary to make the former judgment an estoppel?
25. What must appear in the record of a former judgment?
26. How if the pleadings are general, can the question settled be shown by parol?
27. How as to identity of form of action?
28. In what cases are trover and assumpsit identical in this respect?
29. Against whom can a former judgment be pleaded?
30. How of a foreign judgment?
31. To what kinds of debts does set-off apply?
32. How of a running account between two parties?
33. Is this a common law or statutory defence?
34. How is this defence to be availed of?
35. How of claims for damages?
36. How of claims in equity?
37. Can damages claimed on a contract for quiet enjoyment, be set off in an action for rent?
38. Can a set off be pleaded in an action for unliquidated damages?
39. How can set-off be prevented by plaintiff by the form of action?

40. How of liquidated damages?
41. How of debts of different degrees?
42. What is the practice as to setting off judgments?
43. How of bonds with penalties?
44. Can a debt not yet matured be set off?
45. Can a liability as surety for plaintiff?
46. How of a debt barred by limitations?
47. How if debts are due in different rights?
48. How as to survivor of several?
49. How of executors as to contracts made by themselves?
50. How of trustee and *cestui que trust?*
51. How of nominal and real parties?
52. How as between principal and strangers, with regard to debt of agent?
53. What is the difference between set-off and recoupment?
54. Is the defendant barred by not pleading his set-off?
55. Can non-negotiable note of plaintiff assigned to the defendant be set-off?
56. If the set-off exceed plaintiff's claim, can defendant have judgment for difference?

PARSONS ON CONTRACTS.

PART II, CHAPTER 3, CONTINUED.

1. What does a contract to convey real estate import?
2. What does a "good and sufficient" deed mean?
3. If a contract is to do one of two things who has the choice?
4. Can a contract be optional with one party and binding on the other?
5. When is partial performance a defence *pro tanto?*
6. Is performance after an agreed time a defence?
7. If a thing is to be done in so many days, how are they counted?
8. How when Sunday is the day of performance?

9. If one incapacitates himself from performance before the time agreed, what is the consequence?
10. When is notice required before one is obliged to perform?
11. When is demand or request?
12. When does impossibility excuse?
13. What of covenants to repair?
14. How if contract to do something impossible on its face?
15. How of something simply impossible to the promisor?
16. Would blockade of a port by a foreign power, be the impossibility of delivering goods there, which would excuse?
17. How if our laws forbade the trade?
18. What if a contract is valid when made and the act is made illegal, by a law which is then repealed before time of performance?
19. What is the rule as to dependent and independent covenants when the times of performance are different?
20. How if the party, who is to perform last, disables himself before the time of the other performance?
21. How may a contract be rescinded?
22. Who can exercise the right?
23. How when there has been a partial performance?
24. How if the contract be severable?
25. How if the other party can be put in the same condition as before?
26. Can one rescind without doing this?
27. What exception is there to this?
28. What is the difference between rescinding a contract and suing on it for damages?
29. After rescinding, can one sue for damages?
30. What is accord and satisfaction?
31. Is accord sufficient without satisfaction?
32. How can a sealed instrument be altered?
33. How can a breach be settled?
34. In parol contracts, how can changes be made?
35. How of a new agreement with or without consideration, and in the latter case, executed?

36. If on a new consideration, how far is performance necessary to make accord and satisfaction?
37. How as to a new note, with or without surrender of the old?
38. How does a new executory contract affect remedies on existing debts?
39. How of agreements to dismiss mutual suits, executed?
40. How of collateral security with power of sale, does it suspend action on the original cause?
41. How of specific articles?
42. If the new thing be of no advantage, what?
43. If a parol contract is altered by a new one, before breach, is this an accord and satisfaction?
44. What is agent's or attorney's power to submit to arbitration?
45. Must the submission be mutually binding?
46. What are the general requisites of an award?
47. In what case can it be set aside?
48. A general submission leaves what to the arbitrators?
49. How of mistakes in computation or erroneous assumptions of fact?
50. How of error of judgment in weighing evidence?
51. How of unfairness in proceedings, want of notice, etc.?
52. How ought the umpire to be chosen?
53. Will courts compel a party to perform an agreement to refer?
54. Do they sustain action on such an agreement?
55. How if a party revokes his submission?
56. How long may the right to revoke exist?
57. What would be a revocation?
58. Can submissions under rules of court be revoked?

PARSONS ON CONTRACTS.

Part II, Chapter 3, continued, and Chapter 4.

1. If money is paid under an illegal executory contract can it be recovered?
2. How if performed by the other party? Examples.

3. What of contracts in restraint of trade?
4. What of partial restraints?
5. How of contracts in fraud of revenue laws, domestic and foreign?
6. What wages were illegal at common law?
7. What is champerty and its effect on a contract?
8. What two classes of fraud are there?
9. How far is it necessary that the representation shall be in some material thing?
10. How of misrepresentation by an agent?
11. How far is actual injury necessary?
12. What if the thing represented is true but was not so known to the party?
13. What of a purchase of personalty without the intention of paying for it?
14. What of misrepresentation of value when both parties had equal opportunities of knowing the truth?
15. Is fraud necessary to make a misrepresentation avoid a contract?
16. What difference between representation in and outside of the contract?
17. How is it held in this country as to representation with or without knowledge of their falsity?
18. What of extrinsic matters, as the state of the market, etc.?
19. What of concealments?
20. What of an expression of opinion?
21. In case of fraud, what may a party do in rescinding?
22. What if one act on a fraudulent contract, as to his right afterwards, to rescind?
23. Can one vacate a contract on the ground of his own fraud, as, *e.g.*, set aside a deed because of fraud on his creditors?
24. What difference between law and equity in the relief against fraud?
25. What difference between specialties and simple contracts?
26. In what case will innocent false statements be sufficient ground for setting aside a contract?
27. What is an estoppel?

28. How can it be used?
29. What three general classes are there?
30. What is an estoppel by record?
31. How is one stopped by his own plea?
32. Who are bound by the estoppel of a judgment?
33. What is the rule of mutuality?
34. Who are privies?
35. Who are parties?
36. How of principal and surety?
37. As to what is a judgment an estoppel?
38. How must the estoppel be availed of?
39. What is the effect of not pleading it?
40. What if the declaration is in a general form as in assumpsit?
41. Estoppels by deeds are what?
42. How does estoppel by deed work in case of a grant without title, which is acquired afterwards?
43. Does a mere grant estop one from denying that he had a title?
44. How of deed with general warranty?
45. How as to mortgage with warranty?
46. What statements in deeds are not considered conclusive?
47. How as to payment of the consideration?
48. What are estoppels *in pais?* Examples.
49. What is the extent of the estoppels on a tenant?
50. What is the general principle of equitable estoppel?
51. Is it necessary to plead this estoppel?
52. Give examples of equitable estoppel?
53. Is fraudulent intention essential to make a representation an estoppel?
54. What is the rule as to estoppel against estoppel?
55. Does estoppel arise when an interest passes?

PARSONS ON CONTRACTS.

Part II, Chapter 5.

1. What was the occasion of the Statute of Frauds?
2. What two sections relate to executory contracts? Recite them?
3. What difference is made between the two classes of contracts by the two sections?
4. Is the agreement itself required to be signed?
5. What is a sufficient memorandum of it?
6. What kind of signature is required?
7. When would not signing in the beginning be sufficient?
8. What of printed headings? Pencil signature?
9. Must the memorandum be signed by both parties?
10. Must it be simultaneous with the transaction?
11. Must the agent's authority be in writing?
12. Can one party be agent of another to sign?
13. How of auctioneers?
14. What is the memorandum, etc., at auction sales and in broker's sales?
15. Under the name *agreement* in the Statute, what is included?
16. Can the agreement be made out from several memoranda and how can they be connected?
17. Can parol evidence be allowed to change an agreement required to be in writing?
18. What is the meaning of answering damages by an executor?
19. How where he is residuary legatee and gives bond to pay debts and legacies?
20. How of a promise before one becomes administrator?
21. What is the difference between an original promise and the promise to answer for the debt, etc., of another in the Statute?
22. If two promise jointly and one is known to be accommodation promisor for the other, is it within the Statute?
23. How if the third person's undertaking is extinguished?

24. How if the debt of original debtor is to be kept alive for the benefit of the promisor?
25. How if the promise be made for some special object to the promisor?
26. When I assign a debt in payment of my own, and guarantee it, is this within the Statute?
27. How of a promise of one of several joint debtors to pay the debt?
28. How may the creditor bind himself by his entries and charges?
29. Is a promise to marry within the Statute?
30. Is a promise of advancements to a daughter upon her marriage within the Statute?
31. What is an agreement within the fourth section of the Statute?
32. When is a sale of growing crops within the Statute?
33. How of a sale of underwood, to be cut by buyer, growing trees, etc.?
34. Is a license within the Statute?
35. Or an easement?
36. When is a share of stock in business corporations within the Statute?
37. How if the contract is executed on one side by conveying the land?
38. How as to executory contract, to convey land, when the consideration is paid?
39. What contracts are meant in the fifth clause, not to be performed within one year?
40. If it *may* be so performed, is it within the Statute?
41. How if the contract might, but is not intended or expected to be so performed?
42. What if a contingency might bring the agreement to a close within a year?
43. How if the contract is wholly executed on one side and the price is payable beyond the year?
44. What change does the Statute make as to transfer of title to goods, by sale?
45. What kind of delivery suffices, and is delivery sufficient?

46. Does the Statute apply to contracts to manufacture goods?
47. Is acceptance, to satisfy the Statute, identical with the acceptance which precludes rescission?
48. Is delivery to a carrier sufficient, within the Statute?
49. What part payment will suffice; *e.g.*, will mere giving of credit?
50. When is a contract for future delivery of goods within the Statute?
51. If both parties choose to perform a parol contract within the Statute, can either, or a stranger, afterwards treat it as void?

PARSONS ON CONTRACTS.

Part II, Chapter 6.

1. What limitation of suits existed at common law?
2. To what action does not the act of James I extend?
3. What two views were held as to the Statute?
4. What is the modern view?
5. What is a sufficient promise to take a debt out of the Statute?
6. What is a sufficient implied promise?
7. What of conditional promises?
8. Give examples of acknowledgments by acts?
9. What is the effect of giving credit in account, as to the entire account?
10. What of part payment?
11. What is necessary to give it effect?
12. What of a general payment when one of several debts is disputed?
13. How where one is barred by limitations?
14. What of payment of interest?
15. How of indorsement by creditor?
16. How of an acknowledgment by one partner?
17. How, after dissolution?

18. How of an acknowledgment by one of joint debtors, not partners?
19. To what cases does the exception of accounts between merchants apply?
20. How of accounts between banks?
21. How of accounts between a merchant and his customer?
22. How of stated and closed accounts?
23. From what time is the statutory period counted?
24. How of bill payable at sight? Debt payable on condition?
25. How of account for goods sold?
26. How in case of a surety paying principal's debt?
27. How of claims on co-sureties for contribution?
28. How where one merely pays in instalments?
29. If my agent receives notes for me, from what time does the Statute run against me, from the receipt or payment of the notes?
30. How as to bank notes?
31. What difference does the plaintiff's knowledge that he has a cause of action make?
32. How if he is kept in ignorance by fraud of the other?
33. Does the Statute run from the time of breach or from the date when the injury is received?
34. Against the holder of note, from what time?
35. Against an indorser, as to prior ones?
36. How as to money payable in instalments?
37. How if the whole is due on the first default?
38. How as to trusts?
39. How of an injunction staying suit?
40. Where a new promise is given, from what time does the Statute run?
41. What exceptions are there in the Statute?
42. In case of a minor, when does it begin?
43. When the Statute once begins to run, how if a disability afterwards occurs?
44. How if one is under several disabilities when the cause of action accrues?
45. How if under one disability and others begin afterwards?

46. How if the defendant is abroad when the cause of action accrues?
47. How as to a person who has never been here—an alien?
48. How as to foreign corporations?
49. How if one of several joint debtors is abroad?
50. The term "beyond seas" means what?
51. In case of fraud, when is the cause of action held to accrue?

PARSONS ON CONTRACTS.

Part II, Chapter 7.

1. In what case does the law allow interest without contract?
2. Did the common law allow interest on all overdue debts?
3. In what cases?
4. On book debts, for goods sold, from what time is interest allowed?
5. On account settled? Money lent?
6. On unsettled claims?
7. On note payable on demand?
8. When a note is expressed to be payable with interest at a higher rate than the law gives, without contract, what rate is allowed after maturity?
9. What is usury, and what was the Statute on that subject in England?
10. What was necessary to make a case of usury?
11. How as to further forbearance?
12. Must the usury appear on the face of the contract?
13. How can it be proved?
14. How if stocks, etc., are borrowed at a higher than their real value, with interest on their assumed value?
15. How of a loan of stock, to be returned with all the dividends it earned?
16. How with a loan of stock, with the option to have back the price it sells for, with legal interest on the stock?
17. How with a loan of stock, reserving the dividends?

18. How if the lender is to receive the dividends when above legal interest, and legal interest when they fall below?
19. How if two contracts are made; one to pay principal and legal interest and the other to pay something additional?
20. How when a mere gratuity is given in addition to the legal interest?
21. What if the original debt be legal but a usurious note is given for it?
22. How of an agreement to pay additional interest, if the debt is not paid at maturity?
23. How if I give time to my debtor, in consideration that he pays me the same interest I have to pay some one else?
24. If the note is usurious, can this defence be made against an innocent holder for value?
25. How as to usurious indorsee and his innocent indorsee's rights against maker?
26. How as to collateral securities and substituted notes for an originally usurious debt?
27. How if the new security be given to the innocent transferee of the usurious note?
28. How as to innocent purchaser under the original collateral security?
29. Could the collateral, however, be enforced if objection is made in time?
30. How of a judgment when usury was not pleaded?
31. How of valid notes of third persons given in substitution for or payment of original?
32. Can a contract be purged of usury by a new agreement, and how?
33. Can a second mortgagee set up the objection of usury to the first mortgage?
34. What is the effect of actually taking usury for extending time on a valid contract?
35. What is the difference between defending a suit on the ground of usury and suing to set aside a contract?
36. If usury is paid can the debtor sue to recover it?
37. What is discounting? Is it usury?

38. In what cases is it allowable?
39. Is a charge of more than the legal rate of interest for indorsing or accepting bills usury?
40. Is a deduction of more, in advance, for payment of a debt?
41. How of the building associations?
42. How as to exchange, service, or trouble?
43. How of contracts in which the principal is put at hazard?
44. What is loan on bottomry or respondentia?
45. How of annuities?
46. If one advance money to be used in business for a share of the profits, is it usury if the profits exceed legal interest?
47. Is the purchase of business paper at a large discount usury?*
48. How if I discount a party's own note?
49. How of a note bought from a broker made to raise money on?
50. How if the Statute does not make a note *void* for usury?
51. How where cross-notes are given and one is larger on account of the better credit of the other?
52. Is compound interest usury?
53. Will courts enforce an agreement to pay it?
54. If paid, can it be recovered back?

PARSONS ON CONTRACTS.

Part II, Chapter 8.

1. Is specific performance ever enforced at common law?
2. What is the rule of damages for withholding money?
3. How if special damage resulted from failure to pay?
4. In assumpsit for use and occupation, what is the rule?
5. What is the difference between a penalty and liquidated damages.
6. Which does the court incline to consider it?
7. What rules determine which it is?
8. Are counsel fees, loss of time, etc., allowed for in damages?

9. What is the meaning of giving proof in aggravation or mitigation of damages?
10. What are exemplary or vindictive damages?
11. Are they allowed in case of contract?
12. Can possible, conjectural profits be recovered?
13. In what case can profits be recovered?
14. What does the surety recover before or after paying, where there is a contract by the principal to pay, or a contract to indemnify him?
15. How as to continuing contracts, where instalments are to be paid?
16. How if the contract is entirely broken at once?
17. What is the measure of damages if the agent sells for less than the price directed by the principal?
18. How in case of bad faith?
19. If the agent is directed to ship goods on a certain day and fails, what?
20. How far does the plaintiff's own negligence affect the measure of damages, as, if he could have procured another to do the thing contracted for, at small additional cost?
21. If one whose goods are converted and sold, waive the tort and sue in assumpsit, what is the measure?
22 On replevin bond, what?
23. On contract to deliver goods on a certain day, what is the rule?
24. How when the price has been paid?
25. What is meant by the market price on a certain day?
26. Is it the giving or asking price? At what place?
27. How if goods have fallen in price before the day for delivery?
28. On a sale of real estate, if vendor cannot make good title, what is purchaser's right of recovery?
29. How as to loss of the bargain?
30. How if vendor had falsely represented himself the owner?
31. If buyer of chattels refuses to take, what does seller recover?
32. Is he chargeable with the goods retained?
33. How if the seller sells the goods again?
34. If the goods have been delivered, what is recovered?

35. In case of a sale of land, when purchaser fails to comply, what is the measure of damages?
36. In suit on warranty of chattels retained, what is recovered?
37. In what cases are costs of other actions recovered?
38. How if vendee with warranty resell, with warranty, and is sued and judgment recovered on his warranty?
39. How of costs unnecessarily incurred?
40. Where a debt is payable in money or goods, what is the measure of damages?
41. Where plaintiff has suffered no real damage, ought he to have a judgment?
42. On a covenant of seisin what is the measure?
43. What on covenant of warranty?
44. Where grantee with warranty had granted away with warranty, when is he entitled to sue, if his grantee is evicted?
45. How on covenant against incumbrances?
46. How if he sues before paying them off?

PARSONS ON CONTRACTS.

Part II, Chapter 9.

1. What is a lien?
2. Is it capable of being levied on as property?
3. Is it barred by the Statute of Limitations?
4. Is it destroyed by a set-off?
5. What difference is there between lien on personalty and on realty?
6. Does a lien give a right to sell?
7. What is the difference in a pledge?
8. Is a lien created by contract or law?
9. For what did liens on chattels originally exist?
10. How did general liens arise?
11. Is the finder of a chattel entitled to a lien for expenses, etc.?
12. Can there be a lien without possession?

13. How of a second or third lienor?
14. How far does a general lien interfere with the rights of third persons, *e.g.*, carrier's lien, with consignee, or seller's right of stoppage?
15 Can a lien be transferred separately from the debt?
16. Can one pay the debt for the purpose of getting possession of the property?
17. What effect has surrender of possession?
18. What the transfer of the debt, with possession of the property?
19. What effect has a claim of ownership by the holder of the lien?
20. What if the lienor cause the property to be levied on for his debt?
21. What is the effect of purchase by lienor?
22. If void against creditors, what?
23. What of taking debtor's note?
24. What is the ground of the innkeeper's lien?
25. How lost?
26. Has a livery man a lien?
27. How if employed to train the horse?
28. What is the Common Law lien of the common carrier?
29. How does his general lien arise?
30. What kind of delivery by a seller ends his lien?
31. How if part is delivered in name of whole, or not?
32. How of conditional delivery?
33. How of an order for delivery on bailee?
34. How if goods sold on credit are delivered and returned to seller to be sold on buyer's account?
35. What is the factor's lien?
36. How can the principal effect it?
37. When does the lien of a consignee, agent or factor, begin?
38. What is the banker's lien?
39. Insurance broker's?
40. What that of an attorney-at-law on judgments?
41. What has he before judgment?
42. What on awards?
43. What is the lien of a judgment?

44. What is a lien on debtor's personal property?
45. What are other statutory liens?
46. What is the vendor's lien on land?
47. Against whom is it good?
48. How as to judgment creditor?
49. How as to purchasers with notice? Bankrupt's assignees?
50. Is a receipt for purchase-money conclusive against it?
51. How is this lien waived?
52. Does taking the purchaser's own note amount to it?
53. How is this lien enforced in equity?
54. When does vendee acquire a lien?
55. Has the court a discretion about enforcing this lien, and under what circumstances will it?
56. What was an equitable mortgage?
57. What is the lien of a partner on the partnership stock?
58. What lien has one of several joint-owners?
59. What is a *lis pendens?*
60. How of a *lis pendens* in another jurisdiction than that of the property?

PARSONS ON CONTRACTS.

Part II, Chapter 11.

1. In what case is specific performance enforced at common law?
2. In equity, is it a matter of right or discretion in the court?
3. In what cases will the court refuse to interfere?
4. How if one party would be entitled and the other not, would the court grant it to the latter?
5. Against whom?
6. In favor of whom?
7. How of a contract without consideration?
8. How as to executed *gifts* needing a mere formality?
9. How as to instruments not delivered?
10. How of ante- and post-nuptial agreements to make settlements?

11. How of contracts relating to personalty?
12. In what cases will the court interfere?
13. Will it in regard to a contract to render personal service?
14. How of a contract to execute instruments?
15. How as to contracts for sale of real estate?
16. Can a court compel a conveyance of land out of its jurisdiction?
17. How in suit by vendor if the title is defective?
18. What kind of title must he have?
19. How if the plaintiff removes the objections to his title?
20. By what time must objection to title be removed?
21. Can a purchaser require a warranty?
22. Can he require a conveyance of a part of which the title is good?
23. How does equity regard the vendor from time of sale as to profits, etc.?
24. Is time of the essence of the contract in equity?
25. In what cases is it?
26. How as to parol contracts?
27. In what cases will a court of equity enforce one?
28. What kind of part performance is necessary?
29. What of a confession of the contract in the answer?
30. How if it also rely on the Statute?
31. Is part payment of price a part performance?
32. Preliminary surveys, valuing stock, etc.?
33. What kind of possession is?
34. How of a tenant's previous possession continued?
35. Will marriage be considered part performance of a contract in consideration of marriage?
36. How of a contract partly in writing and partly parol?
37. In what cases does equity give compensation in damages?
38. How are they ascertained?
39. How in favor of vendee, in case of part performance?
40. How if contractor dies?
41. How if he had contracted to devise?
42. How if complainant is incapable of being coerced—as a minor—will defendant be compelled to perform?
43. Or if performance by plaintiff is impossible?

44. How if minor sue for specific performance when he comes of age?
45. How if plaintiff's performance in future is improbable because of present insolvency?
46. How if plaintiff has partly performed and cannot wholly?
47. Can a married woman make a binding contract which the court can enforce?
48. How as to her separate property?
49. How if the husband contract that the wife shall convey?
50. What relief could be given in such a case?
51. What will induce a court of equity to give relief which would not be a defence at common law?
52. What relief can a court of equity give as to deeds of trust?

PARSONS ON CONTRACTS.

Part II, Chapter 12.

1. At common law what rights had a debtor in the way of preferring creditors?
2. How in equity?
3. What are the differences between bankruptcy and insolvent laws?
4. What does the constitution provide as to bankrupt laws?
5. Does it prevent the States from passing insolvent laws?
6. What effect is given to a foreign bankrupt discharge in the State where the contract is made?
7. How of a discharge at the place of the contract?
8. Does an assignment in bankruptcy carry effects abroad?
9. How as against foreign creditors attaching?
10. How if the assignee once reduces the effects into possession?
11. Who can become a voluntary bankrupt and how?
12. Who are embraced under the term "persons?"
13. What does "residence" mean?
14. What is the effect of filing the petition?

15. What is the debtor required to state?
16. What is the proceeding upon the filing of the petition?
17. What is the nature of the proceeding?
18. What is necessary to give the court jurisdiction?
19. How is assignee to be appointed?
20. How may the estate be settled up otherwise than by the assignee?
21. What are acts of involuntary bankruptcy?
22. What are the two kinds of assignments that amount to bankruptcy?
23. What is a trader?
24. What is commercial paper?
25. Is assignment for benefit of all creditors an act of bankruptcy?
26. What is the nature of the proceeding in involuntary bankruptcy?
27. What may the debtor do in answer to the petition of the creditors?
28. What is the judgment of the court on the hearing?
29. What are assignee's duties?
30. What as to incumbered property?
31. Can the property be sold free of incumbrance, and if so by what proceeding?
32. What choice of proceedings has the secured creditor?
33. What is the assignee's duties as to fraudulent assignments?
34. Can he purchase the trust property?
35. What is the effect of taking a lease under the assignment?
36. What is assignee's right and duty if the lease is an unprofitable one?
37. What is the effect of adjudication on pending suits?
38. What of the filing of the petition?
39. What is the power of the assignee as to negotiable securities?
40. What as to compromises?
41. What property passes by the assignment?
42. What if a devise to an insolvent goes into effect after proceedings commenced?
43. What if the inheritance comes after discharge?
44. What of bankrupt's interest in his wife's estate?

45. What personal estate passes?
46. What of leases and policies not assignable?
47. Does such assignment avoid such leases or insurance?
48. How as to wife's choses in action?
49. How if husband dies before assignee reduces them into possession?
50. What of a partner's interest?
51. Can stoppage *in transitu* be exercised by assignee?
52. If assignee elects not to receive a burdensome lease, what becomes of it?
53. How if indorsement on bills made after bankruptcy, to innocent parties?
54. How of collection of accommodation paper?
55. What property is exempt from the assignment?
56. When does bankrupt's power over his property cease?
57. Within what time are assignments before bankruptcy void, and what assignments are so?
58. What debts are provable?
59. How as to rents accruing after bankruptcy when the assignee does not take the lease?
60. What claims can be resisted by the assignee?
61. How as to claims founded on fraud to which the debtor was a party and which he could not resist?
62. How of torts?
63. Can he plead limitations or rely on the Statute of Frauds?
64. Are judgments conclusive against the assignee?
65. How of claims for damages reduced to judgment?
66. How is the liability of debtor to a fund of which he is trustee to be proven?
67. What is the effect of the discharge?
68. To what debts is a discharge a bar?
69. How if the debt is not proved through accident?
70. In what cases is a discharge not a bar to future suits?
71. In case of voluntary bankruptcy what amount of assets is necessary to entitle to discharge?

PARSONS ON CONTRACTS.

PART II, CHAPTER 13.

1. What is a contract within the meaning of the Constitution of the United States?
2. In what case was this question discussed and decided?
3. What other important point was decided in that case?
4. Does this rule prevent legislation indirectly affecting the value of property?
5. How as to grants of powers, etc., to municipal corporation?
6. What was decided in Darmouth College *vs.* Woodward?
7. Does a compact between States come within the protection of the Constitution?
8. Does the Constitution conflict with the common law rule that one legislature cannot tie the hands of subsequent ones?
9. How if a right of alteration is reserved in a charter?
10. Does a grant of important franchises prevent a State from granting others, when public interest requires it, that interfere with the first?
11. What important case decided this question?
12. How of a grant with express contract against future taxation?
13. How of a grant of exclusive privileges to the exclusion of competition?
14. In case of great necessity could such grant be interfered with, and how?
15. Is a corporate franchise the subject of this right of eminent domain?
16. How can an exemption from taxation be removed?
17. Is marriage a contract within the constitutional protection?
18. What is a divorce now considered to be?
19. What is the effect of a discharge in bankruptcy in a State on previous debts there?
20. In what case decided?
21. What effect as to subsequent debts?

22. What effect has such a discharge in another State than the place of contract?
23. Suppose a law took away all remedies without professing to discharge the debt, would it be void?
24. How of stay laws and others exempting property from sale under execution?
25. How of exemption laws?
26. How as to those stay laws, etc., as respects subsequent debts?
27. Do changes in the Acts of limitation come within the prohibition?
28. How as to laws of a police character, as regulating sales of intoxicating liquors, lotteries, etc., after licenses are given, with or without payment of consideration?

BYLES ON BILLS.

CHAPTERS 1, 2, 3, AND 4.

1. Of what does commercial paper consist?
2. To whom is the invention of bills of exchange attributed?
3. What were promissory notes at common law?
4. What is a bill of exchange?
5. What are the names of the different parties to it?
6. How is it transferred?
7. What is indorsement?
8. What is the theory of bills?
9. Who is principal debtor after acceptance?
10. How if for accommodation?
11. How does commercial paper differ as to consideration from specialties and other simple contracts?
12. Were notes and bills the subject of larceny?
13. Could they be levied upon by execution?
14. What is a promissory note?
15. What its difference from a bill?

16. How do the parties to the two resemble each other as to liability?
17. What did the Statute of Anne provide?
18. What if the instrument be conditional?
19. How if payable out of a particular fund?
20. How if payable otherwise than in money?
21. How as to current funds? Exchange?
22. How if the memorandum as to the fund does not form part of the note?
23. How far must the sum be certain?
24. What certainty is necessary as to the time of payment?
25. How of a note payable at death?
26. Can one make a note to himself? To himself and another?
27. With another to himself?
28. Is a note payable in instalments good?
29. How if on one default the whole becomes payable?
30. How as to days of grace?
31. Can it be indorsed over for less than its face?
32. When is a note joint?
33. How if in the singular but signed by several?
34. What makes it joint and several?
35. For what purposes is it joint and for what several?
36. Can holder select several out of more to sue jointly?
37. Can one of joint promisors show that he was surety only?
38. What are bank notes?
39. What are bank checks?
40. What difference between the latter and an inland bill?
41. When is a post-dated or antedated check payable?
42. If a check is payable on a day certain, is it entitled to grace?
43. What is the banker's obligation?
44. What difference between check and bill as to being overdue and taken free from equities?
45. What claim has the holder on the banker?
46. When has he a right of action?
47. Is the holder bound to the same diligence in presenting a check as a bill?
48. What is his duty?

49. When must a check be presented in order to charge the drawer, in case of refusal of drawee, where all are in the same town, and how when they are in different towns?
50. What difference between drawer and indorser when the check is circulated?
51. How if drawer has no funds?
52. What is the effect of marking the check "good?"
53. What of stopping payment by the drawer?
54. What is crossing a check with the banker's name?
55. Of what is a check *prima facie* evidence against drawer?
56. If check is paid by the bank, of what is it evidence?
57. When is a check a good tender?
58. Is it a good payment?
59. What is necessary to make it evidence of payment?
60. What if bill or note be given up for a check?
61. What would be the effect of the drawer's death?
62. What of payment of a raised or altered check?
63. What if drawer had left bank checks with an agent which are fraudulently filled up?
64. How must check be signed by joint depositors?
65. Is a check the subject of *donatio mortis causa?*
66. How as to check of third person?
67. Is a due bill a promissory note?

BYLES ON BILLS.

Chapter 5.

1. Who are capable of being parties to bills and notes?
2. Who can act as agents in regard to them?
3. How must agent sign?
4. How if he signs in his own name?
5. Does a general employment authorize agent to indorse and accept, etc.?
6. How is power to sign, etc., construed?

7. How is taker affected by notice of agency?
8. How if he takes overdue paper from agent?
9. Can agent pledge for individual debts?
10. How if taker of such pledge knows of the agency?
11. How as to bill brokers?
12. Is the holder of a bill bound to take agent's acceptance?
13. If not satisfied of his authority, what may he do?
14. If agent executes in his own name, can principal be sued?
15. How ought a note to be executed to make it bind the principal?
16. How if agent execute without authority?
17. How if innocently, as in ignorance of principal's death?
18. Where agent holds bills, etc., to collect, what is his responsibility?
19. What is a banker's?
20. What is the general power of a partner as to commercial paper?
21. How when there is a private agreement limiting the power to one or more?
22. Can suit be brought on a note by a partner to his firm?
23. How avoid the difficulty?
24. By what signature by one partner is the firm made party to paper?
25. How if he sign his own name, though the proceeds are to go to the firm?
26. Can one partner give a joint *and several* note to bind the firm?
27. Can he give the firm note for his private business?
28. Or a guaranty of a note or accommodation paper?
29. What effect has the accepting of one partner's paper on the obligation of the firm?
30. After dissolution can one partner bind by a new note?
31. Can he indorse a bill owned by the firm?
32. If one deal with an executor or administrator whose letters are afterwards revoked, is he protected?
33. What are the powers of executors or administrators as to testator's bills and notes?

34. What the effect of appointing acceptor executor of holder?
35. How if the executor be one of several debtors, or principal debtor, as acceptor?
36. How in this country?
37. How must and can an executor sue on a note given him for a debt to the testator?
38. What counts may he join?
39. What if executor gives notes or indorses notes?
40. What is the rule as to joining demands against executor?
41. What contracts may an infant not make?
42. What is the difference between void and voidable contracts?
43. What of his bills and notes in trade?
44. What if given for necessaries?
45. Are they void or voidable?
46. Can an infant draw or indorse so as to give an action against acceptor?
47. Can an infant be sued for fraud?
48. In joint contract of infant and adult how should suit be brought?
49. What of the notes of a lunatic?
50. Can a married woman give notes or bills?
51. How in case of separate estate?
52. What becomes of paper owned by her at marriage?
53. What is a reduction to possession?
54. How as to husband's assignment, in solvency or bankruptcy?
55. Is payment of a note owned by a *feme covert*, to her, a good payment?
56. What of notes from wife to husband?
57. What power has a corporation to execute commercial paper?

BYLES ON BILLS.

CHAPTERS 6, 7 8, AND 10.

1. On what must a bill or note be written?
2. How of the writing?

3. Is date or place essential?
4. How of signature?
5. If no time of payment is stated, when is it payable?
6. What is payment at one or more usances, or at half usance?
7. What does "after sight" mean in a note and in a bill?
8. When a bill is made to a fictitious person and his name indorsed, what is the effect?
9. What if payee's name be left blank?
10. Are the words "value received" necessary, or any other consideration, to be expressed?
11. Is a bill payable to drawee's order, but signed by him, good?
12. Where must the signature be?
13. If drawee's name is omitted but some one accepts it, is it good?
14. Can a bill on one be accepted by another?
15. How if drawn on one and, in case of his absence, on another?
16. How if drawn on three and accepted by two?
17. How if drawn on himself?
18. In favor of himself?
19. Is a non-negotiable bill or note a good bill or note?
20. How if endorsed by payee?
21. If doubtful whether an instrument is a bill or note how may holder treat it?
22. What is a bill drawn on the drawer himself?
23. How if drawn on a wife?
24. If one indorsed order on a bond to pay it to a third person, is it a good bill?
25. If a note is signed A or else B, is it good?
26. If payable to A, B or C?
27. If drawn on a joint fund?
28. How of parol evidence modifying the obligation inferred by law?
29. May a bill be delivered as an escrow?
30. What must be averred and proved in regard to consideration of other simple contracts and what of notes, and what if defendant impeach the consideration?
31. What of accommodation bills?

32. By what proof can the onus be thrown on the plaintiff of showing a consideration?
33. Between any immediate parties, what can be shown as to consideration?
34. How as to indorsees without value?
35. How of indorsees for value, but with notice?
36. How if with notice, but under a prior party holding without notice and for value?
37. What amounts to notice?
38. Will suspicious circumstances be sufficient?
39. What would be constructive notice?
40. Will a pre-existing debt be a sufficient consideration to protect a holder?
41. How of a fluctuating balance?
42. How of a prior debt of a third person?
43. What if holder knows the want of consideration between maker and payee?
44. What in case of accommodation notes?
45. How if less than the face of them be given?
46. How if indorsee knows that the notes are wilfully misapplied by payee?
47. Can partial failure of consideration be shown in defence?
48. Can damages be shown in reduction of claim on a note?
49. How does fraud affect the note?
50. How illegality in the consideration?
51. How as to *bona fide* holders?
52. How as to renewals of originals given for illegal consideration?

BYLES ON BILLS.

Chapters 11 and 12.

1. What is the effect of indorsement by payee of non-negotiable notes?
2. How is paper payable to bearer transferred?

3. How notes payable to order of A B?
4. How if payable to A for the use of B?
5. How many kinds of indorsements?
6. What is the effect of a blank indorsement?
7. What is the effect of a full indorsement?
8. How of form of indorsement—omission of the word order?
9. What is a restrictive indorsement?
10. How can a blank be made a full indorsement?
11. If the first indorsement is blank, what is the effect of subsequent indorsements?
12. What can a holder do where the subsequent indorsements are full? In blank?
13. What is a qualified indorsement?
14. Can indorser enlarge his common law liability?
15. What is a conditional indorsement?
16. What is the contract of the indorser?
17. What does an indorsement admit?
18. What are the indorsee's rights?
19. What is his remedy if the party transferring to him has omitted to indorse?
20. What if a bill comes back to the first indorser?
21. How if indorsee have notice of a trust?
22. How in case of restrictive indorsement?
23. What are the rights of transferee by delivery?
24. To what kind of defence is the holder of overdue paper subject?
25. What is the difference between taking an overdue acceptance and taking a bill not accepted, without notice?
26. When will a note or bill be presumed to have been transferred?
27. When is a bank check overdue?
28. When a note payable on demand?
29. If a note be paid before due and circulated again, is it good in the hands of the indorsee?
30. How if paid at maturity?
31. How if a stranger pays a note in bank at maturity?

32. If a bill be partially paid at maturity, what is the consequence to a new taker?
33. How if it comes back to the acceptor and is reissued by him?
34. Can it be indorsed for less than the whole amount due?
35. What would be the effect of such an indorsement?
36. How must an indorsement be made after death, bankruptcy, or marriage?
37. How does a pledge of bills, etc., differ from a pledge of other things?
38. Are notes, etc., the subject of larceny?
39. Could they be taken in execution?
40. Are they the subject of *donatio mortis causa?*

Chapter 12.

41. What is the difference between bills and notes, as to presentment for acceptance?
42. When may a bill be presented for acceptance?
43. How of bills payable so long after sight?
44. How of promissory notes so payable?
45. In what cases must a holder present for acceptance a time bill?
46. *When* must a sight bill be presented?
47. *When* a time bill?
48. *Where?*
49. What if drawee is incompetent, dead, bankrupt, or absconded?

BYLES ON BILLS.

Chapters 13, 14, and 15.

1. What is an acceptance?
2. Has payee any right of action against drawer before acceptance?
3. When an acceptance is payable at a banker's what is the latter's duty?

4. What if the bill omit the name of drawee and some one accepts?
5. If he is named, can any one else accept?
6. What if another writes his name under?
7. Can there be a blank acceptance?
8. Under what circumstance can there be an acceptance of a non-existing bill?
9. Does this apply to sight bills? Why?
10. Was a verbal acceptance good?
11. What kind of bills were considered accepted as soon as drawn?
12. What of acceptance after maturity?
13. When will an acceptance be presumed to have been made?
14. What form is a sufficient acceptance?
15. Is mere detention an acceptance?
16. Is a holder bound to receive a verbal acceptance?
17. Or a conditional one?
18. What must he do if he takes a conditional acceptance?
19. Can the condition be shown by parol?
20. What if an acceptance vary from the bill?
21. What of an acceptance payable at a particular place?
22. After acceptance, what is acceptor's relation to other parties?
23. What distinction is there as to releases, between commercial paper and other contracts?
24. How of taking other security, as the separate note of one partner?
25. What does acceptance admit?
26. How, if drawn payable to drawer's order, as to his indorsement?
27. How, ordinarily, is a demand to be made for payment?
28. Must it be personal?
29. At what place must it be?
30. How, if made payable at a particular bank, as to acceptor or maker and as to drawer or indorser?
31. How in case of bankruptcy, death, or removal?
32. How as to guarantors?

33. When a bill is made payable so many days after date, is the day of date excluded?
34. What does "month" mean?
35. What are days of grace?
36. On what day is payment to be demanded?
37. How in case of holidays intervening?
38. Bills on demand and checks are to be demanded when?
39. Promissory notes on demand?
40. Bank notes?
41. How when both pass through several hands?
42. At what time of day should a demand be made?
43. How if the bank where the note is payable is the holder?
44. What circumstances will excuse want of presentment for payment?
45. How if drawer has no funds in drawee's hands?
46. How if he have a right to expect payment?
47. How of acceptance for accommodation of any of the parties?
48. How of waiver of the laches?
49. How if a party has received security or indemnity against loss?
50. Will knowledge by drawer of acceptor's inability to pay excuse?
51. Who is entitled to receive payment?
52. What would be a payment out of the usual course of business?
53. If a note is payable to order, what of payment to holder through a forged indorsement?
54. What payment will discharge a note?
55. What is the effect of part payment by a drawee to the holder?
56. What of payment by a stranger?
57. What is the effect of payment at maturity?
58. Before maturity?
59. On payment, what is maker's right to possession of note?
60. Indorser's?
61. How if acceptor's check be taken and not paid?
62. How should payment be made?

63. Will a legacy of debtor to holder be a payment?
64. What rights does payment by drawer or indórser give him?

BYLES ON BILLS.

Chapters 16 to 22 inclusive.

1. What was the common law rule as to release or satisfaction of contracts?
2. What is the presumption when a negotiable note is taken for a debt?
3. What is the effect of taking a higher security?
4. Does recovery of judgment against one affect the recourse against the others?
5. What is the effect of taking a note or bill on account of previous debt?
6. Is a covenant not to sue pleadable as a release?
7. How if it is not to sue for limited time?
8. How as to such covenant to one of joint debtors?
9. Who are principals and who sureties on commercial paper?
10. What is the effect of release to principal?
11. What on prior parties of release to subsequent ones?
12. What kind of agreement of forbearance with principal will discharge the surety?
13. How if judgment is to be entered in case of default?
14. How if the agreement is void under the Statute of Frauds?
15. What is the effect of tender after maturity?
16. What difference betwėen release to one of several joint promisors and to principal?
17. What of surrender or loss of collaterals by holder?
18. What if holder release maker's person or goods taken in execution?
19. What effect has discharge in bankruptcy of maker?
29. What if bill be given up for a new one of drawee taken before acceptance?

21. When will giving time to acceptor not discharge the other parties?
22. When will discharge of surety discharge principal?
23. Are successive indorsers co-sureties entitled to contribution from each other?
24. How as to joint drawers or indorsers?
25. On refusal of acceptance, what is the holder's next duty?
26. What is a protest?
27. By whom is it to be drawn up?
28. What paper must be protested?
29. In the absence of a notary, by whom?
30. When must protest be made?
31. What is protest *for better security?*
32. What excuses omission to protest?
33. What not?
34. Is protest of inland bills or notes evidence of dishonor?
35. What is an acceptance *supra protest?*
36. Can more than one accept supra protest?
37. Can drawee after refusing to accept, accept supra protest?
38. Is holder obliged to take acceptance supra protest?
39. What if he does?
40. To whom is acceptor for honor bound, and against whom may he have recourse?
41. What does his acceptance admit?
42. What is payment for honor?
43. How is it done?
44. What rights does it give the party?
45. What is the difference between guarantor and indorser as to notice?
46. Is knowledge by a party sufficient without formal notice?
47. What must the notice contain?
48. Must it be in writing?
49. How must notice be sent to non-resident parties?
50. What proofs of notice may be given?
51. How must it be addressed to a person in a large town?
52. How where the party resides in the country?
53. Can it be sent by private messenger?

54. If indorser lives in the same town where the bill is payable, where and how must notice be sent?
55. If a party direct a notice to be sent to a place distant from his home, how?
56. When must it be given in the same town?
57. How, if sent to another town?
58. What right has each indorser, receiving notice?
59. How of a bank holding for collection?
60. By whom must notice be given?
61. How if a party has been discharged?
62. If one indorser give notice can the holder avail himself of it?
63. What is the duty of a creditor holding as collateral?
64. To whom should notice be given?
65. What is the effect of notifying one and his notifying the next, etc.?
66. What if one in the line fails?
67. Can extra diligence of one make up for the fault of others?
68. In case of bankruptcy or death, how is notice to be given?
69. How as to partners?
70. How as to joint indorsers, not partners?
71. Is one transferring by delivery entitled to notice?
72. What difference is there between transfer in payment of previous debt and transfer in payment for goods?
73. Is guarantor entitled to notice?
74. If indorser binds himself by bond, will his discharge on the note discharge the bond?
75. What is the consequence of omission to notify drawer and indorsers?
76. Is the indorser, not notified, discharged from the original consideration?
77. Can one of several so discharged pay the bill and sue the others?
78. What will excuse want of notice to drawer?
79. When will absence of funds in drawer's hands not be an excuse?
80. Does it dispense with notice to indorsers?

81. How of a shifting balance in accounts between drawer and drawee?
82. How is the holder's laches waived?
83. What is necessary to make the waiver good?
84. What of his legal ignorance?

BYLES ON BILLS.

Chapters 28 to 33 inclusive.

1. Does a finder acquire property in a lost bill payable to bearer?
2. How of *bona fide* taker from him?
3. Does loss dispense with demand, etc.?
4. If a note be in defendant's hands, what is plaintiff's course?
5. Can recovery be on a lost bill or note, and what difference between negotiable and non-negotiable?
6. What difference between maker and indorser?
7. What is the relief given in equity?
8. What is the effect of taking a note on account of an existing debt?
9. How if taken at the time for goods sold?
10. What effect if the note is taken only as collateral?
11. What is a creditor's duty who takes the note or bill of a third person?
12. What if he fails to present and notify?
13. What if he passes off the paper to a third person?
14. How are sealed instruments affected by taking note or bill?
15. In what case will a new note be presumed a satisfaction of a prior debt?
16. What is the effect of taking a note, on a lien?
17. What if the note be dishonored?
18. What is the object of sets of foreign bills?
19. What is the condition on which each is payable?
29. On transfer, what must each indorsee do?

21. What is the effect of paying one?
22. How if they get into different innocent persons' hands?
23. By what law are the contracts of the different parties to commercial paper governed?
24. Where does the drawer and where the indorser promise to pay?
25. What law determines whether protest and notice shall be necessary and as to the form?
26. By what law is the question of grace determined?
27. Interest?
28. Stamps?
29. Limitations?
30. Set-off?
31. Who is entitled to sue on a bill?
32. What if plaintiff transfer before or after action brought?
33. Whom may the holder sue?
34. The indorser who pays him?
35. Can an indorser sue intermediate parties in name of last indorsee, on payment to him?
36. How of costs against acceptor?
37. In trover for a bill what does plaintiff recover?
38. How if the bill is surrendered?
39. If judgment is paid, what becomes of the note?
40. What is re-exchange and the right of the holder in regard to it?
41. Against whom has he this right?
42. What is the legal par of exchange?
43. What is the real rate of exchange?

www.ingramcontent.com/pod-product-compliance
Lightning Source LLC
Chambersburg PA
CBHW021119270326
41929CB00009B/948

* 9 7 8 3 3 3 7 1 7 9 9 1 5 *